BEGINNING **BANJO**

GW00759908

The Complete 5-String Banjo Method

Beginning • Intermediate • Mastering

NED LUBERECKI

ONLINE ACCESS INCLUDED

  To access audio and video,
visit: **alfred.com/redeem**

Enter this unique code:

00-44932_17803242

Alfred Music
P.O. Box 10003
Van Nuys, CA 91410-0003
alfred.com

ISBN-10: 1-4706-3037-0 (Book & Online Audio/Video)
ISBN-13: 978-1-4706-3037-9 (Book & Online Audio/Video)

Cover photo by Ryan McGuire of gratisography.com
Interior photos by Scott Simontacchi, unless otherwise credited

CONTENTS

ABOUT THE AUTHOR

A professional noted for his dazzling technique, originality, and broad sense of humor, Ned Luberecki has played for over a decade with Chris Jones & The Night Drivers. His resume includes stints with Paul Adkins & The Borderline Band, Gary Ferguson, Radio Flyer, and the Rarely Herd. Ned is a popular banjo instructor at some of the most renowned instructional camps in the United States, Canada, and Europe—as well as at his studio in Nashville, TN, where he gives private lessons both in person and online. Ned is also a broadcaster on SiriusXM's Bluegrass Junction channel, where he hosts the popular newgrass/progressive bluegrass shows Derailed and More Banjo Sunday.

ABOUT THE MEDIA

The video contains valuable demonstrations of the instructional material in this book. You will get the best results by following along with your book as you watch these video segments. The symbol to the left appears next to every song, example, or lesson in the book with an accompanying video demonstration. Example numbers appear above the symbol when applicable. Audio tracks of the musical examples files are also included and can be streamed or downloaded.

See page 1 for instructions for accessing the media.

INTRODUCTION

Welcome to *Beginning Banjo*, the first book in the *Complete 5-String Banjo Method*, a series designed to take you from the absolute beginning level to as far as you want to go! When you are done with this book, move on to *Intermediate Banjo* and then *Mastering Banjo*.

The 5-string banjo has come a long way—from its early plantation and vaudeville days, through the folk music boom, and then gaining popularity in bluegrass and country music—to today, where it is heard in many styles of music, including classical, jazz, and even rock.

Many of the techniques used in 5-string banjo playing are rooted in folk, bluegrass, and country music, so much of the music contained in this book will be from those genres. While a deep knowledge of those styles is not necessary to learn to play the banjo, some familiarity with banjo music is certainly helpful. In addition to working with the lessons in this book and on the accompanying video, listen to as much banjo music as possible. Knowing what great banjo playing sounds like will not only inspire you to practice but also help to get the sound "inside your head," so you'll know when you've got it right.

THIS BOOK IS FOR THE 5-STRING BANJO

If your banjo has five strings, you've got the right book! The 5-string banjo is the most popular, but there are also four-string and six-string banjos. Four-string banjos are commonly associated with Dixieland jazz and played with a *flat pick* (a small, thin teardrop-shaped device usually made out of plastic used to strike a string). Two popular four-string models are the *tenor banjo* (short neck) and the *plectrum banjo* (longer neck). The six-string banjo is tuned and played like a guitar, so while the body style may look like a banjo, it's essentially a guitar.

WHAT YOU WILL LEARN IN THIS BOOK

- How to hold, pick, fret, and strum the banjo
- How to read tablature (TAB)
- How to play basic chords in open position
- How to play rolls (fingerpicking patterns used to play the banjo)
- How to play songs using bluegrass-style licks
- The basics of music theory
- Basic melodic-style banjo playing
- Basic clawhammer- or frailing-style banjo playing
- Banjo maintenance and setup, including how to change strings

WHO THIS BOOK IS FOR

Beginning Banjo is written for the complete beginner with no musical experience necessary. If you have played another string instrument, especially a guitar or mandolin, you'll find that some of the same techniques will apply. However, use caution when skipping over sections on techniques you think you might already know. Because of the unique tuning and playing style of the 5-string banjo, some familiar techniques may differ in subtle ways.

AFTER BEGINNING BANJO

Once you complete this book, you'll be ready for *Intermediate Banjo*, and then, after that, you can move on to *Mastering Banjo*. The skills you gain in *Beginning Banjo* will enable you to learn songs on your own and get you started with jamming with other musicians, which is where the real fun is! The appendix at the end of this book provides resources—such as bluegrass organizations, magazines, music camps, and festivals—and lists banjo players whose playing you should hear.

CHAPTER 1

Getting Started——You and Your Banjo

LESSON 1: PARTS OF THE BANJO

Let's get started by getting familiar with your instrument. There might be a few differences between your banjo and the one below, but, for now, as long as your banjo has five strings and is in tune, we're in business! For more information on the different varieties of banjos, check out Chapter 10, beginning on page 83. Take a look below for the various parts of the banjo.

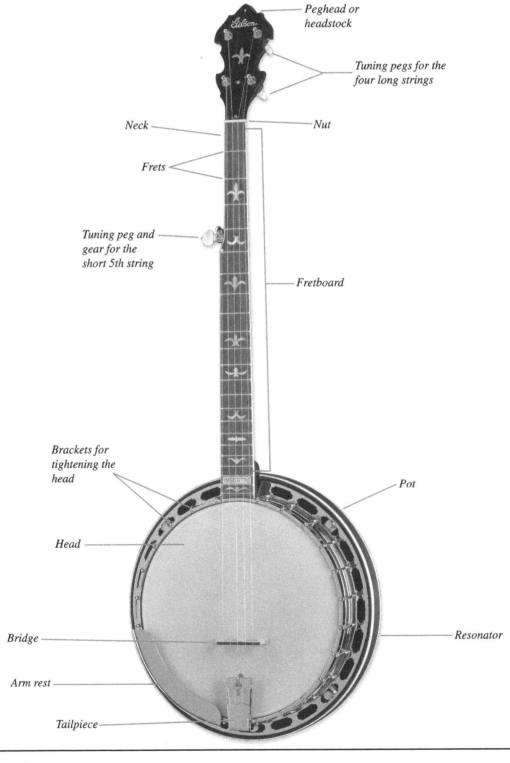

Peghead or headstock

Tuning pegs for the four long strings

Neck — — Nut

Frets

Tuning peg and gear for the short 5th string

Fretboard

Brackets for tightening the head

Pot

Head

Bridge

Resonator

Arm rest

Tailpiece

The banjo is tuned to a *G chord* (a chord is a group of notes, or musical sounds, played together and each chord has a letter name—more on this later). In other words, unlike the guitar or mandolin, playing the banjo strings *open* (without pressing any strings to the fretboard) sounds a chord. The chart below relates the pitches of the open banjo strings to a piano keyboard and shows how you can tune the banjo by matching the *pitch* (highness or lowness of sound) of a *fretted* string (a string you are pressing into the fretboard) to the sound of next open string. This is called *relative tuning*.

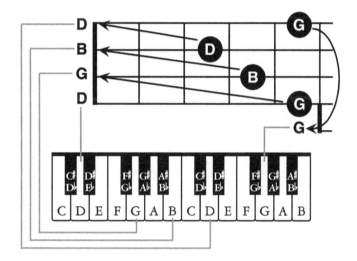

ELECTRONIC TUNERS

Another way to tune your banjo is with an *electronic tuner*. Available online and at most music stores, an electronic tuner senses what pitch is being played and has an indicator showing whether you need to tune the string higher (when the pitch is *flat,* or too low) or lower (when the pitch is *sharp,* or too high) to reach the desired pitch. Some tuners sense sound with a built in microphone, while others clip on to the instrument and sense vibrations. There are even tuner apps available for your smartphone or computer. With a little practice, electronic tuners can be easy to use and are very accurate, but it's still a good idea to learn relative tuning. It will help develop your ear, which will help you learn to play by ear (the ability to learn to play a song just by hearing it) to become a better musician.

The photos below show the proper way to hold the banjo while seated and while standing. In order to play the banjo standing up, you'll need to use a *banjo strap* (see below). Although some players like to use a strap while seated, you can play the banjo sitting down without a strap. We'll discuss how to choose and attach a banjo strap later (see page 91).

Most folks find it more comfortable to place the banjo strap over their left shoulder, however some prefer the "old-time" method of hanging the banjo over their right shoulder. This method was adopted back when everyone wore hats on stage; with the banjo going over your right shoulder, you could strap it on without removing your hat. Try both ways and see which is more comfortable for you.

A NOTE FOR THE LEFTIES

As you may have already noticed, most banjos are made for right-handed players. And since the 5th-string tuning peg is on the top side of the neck, restringing a banjo to be left-handed is not as easy to do as it is with a guitar (you'd have to replace the entire neck!). Left-handed banjos are available, but they can be hard to come by. The decision to play right- or left-handed is one that you will have to make on your own, but consider this: because the banjo is fingerpicked, quite a bit of dexterity is required of both hands and it could be to your advantage to simply learn to play on a right-handed banjo. After all, they don't make left-handed pianos or left-handed computer keyboards, and lots of lefties learn to play the piano and type. If you already have a left-handed banjo, then simply reverse the right- and left-hand terms used throughout this method.

The banjo is played with *fingerpicks*. Unlike flat picks, which are used to play the guitar and mandolin and held between the thumb and finger, fingerpicks are worn on the ends of the fingers and the thumb pick is wrapped around the end of the thumb, allowing one hand to pick several strings at once. Generally, three fingerpicks are used: one on the thumb, and one each for the middle and index fingers. Fingerpicks are most commonly made of metal and can be bent to fit the fingers. Of course, it's possible to play the banjo with your bare fingers, but in order to get a loud, full sound, picks are necessary. They may take a little getting used to, but keep practicing with them and they'll soon feel as comfortable as a pair of old shoes.

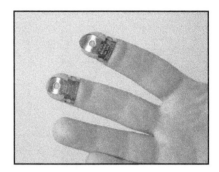
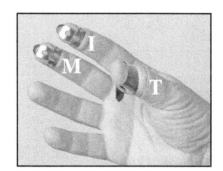

Thumb picks are most often made of plastic and are worn as shown. Look for a thumb pick that fits tightly so that it doesn't spin around easily on your thumb but loose enough that it isn't uncomfortable.

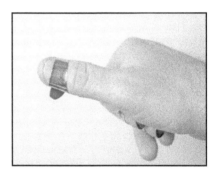

There are many different brands and styles of fingerpicks and thumb picks, and part of the fun in learning the banjo is experimentation! Go ahead and try out some different kinds, but remember that the pick doesn't make the picker!

Position your right hand as shown, with your arm on the armrest (see Parts of the Banjo, page 6) and the ring and pinky fingers resting on the banjo head just in front of the bridge. (If your banjo doesn't have an armrest, don't worry. Just position your arm as if it does.) Keeping those two fingers planted on the head will help to steady your hand and increase your accuracy. You should be able to hold the banjo steady with your right hand and arm only, leaving your left hand to move freely without gripping the neck.

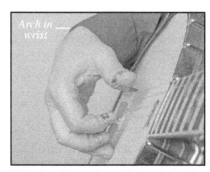

Right hand from above. Notice the arch in the wrist.

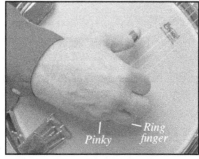

Right hand from front. Notice the placement of the ring and pinky fingers.

We change the pitch of a string by making its vibrating length shorter or longer, which is done by pressing it onto a *fret* (see Parts of the Banjo, page 6); this is called *fretting*. To fret a note, hold down the string just behind (to the left of) the fret you wish to play. If you hold the string down directly on top of the fret, your finger will mute the note. If you place your finger too far behind the fret, you may not get enough pressure to make a clear note. Also, try to fret the strings with just the tips of your fingers, with your fingertip pointing straight down (as opposed to slightly sideways) in order to avoid touching strings other than the one you are playing. The fingers of your left hand are numbered as shown.

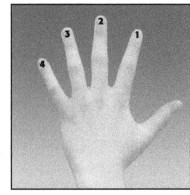
Left-hand finger numbers.

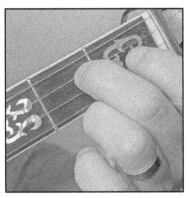
Too far from fret.

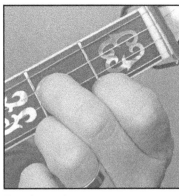
Too close to fret.

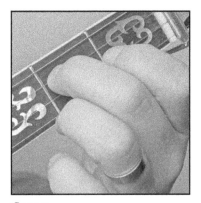
Correct.

When fretting a note, your left thumb should be behind the neck (not wrapped around the top) and your wrist should be slightly bent so that the palm of your hand is not touching.

Correct thumb position.

Incorrect thumb position.

The Banjo Neck Is Not a Handle
The first time you sat down with your banjo in your lap you probably noticed that, since the body of the banjo is round, the neck started to drift down toward the floor. The natural thing to do is hold the neck up with your left hand, right? *Don't do it!* Try to get used to holding the banjo in your lap by using your right arm on the armrest and your two right-hand fingers planted on the banjo head. A strap can also be helpful to keep the banjo in playing position. Holding the neck up with your left hand not only limits the mobility and agility of your left hand, it's also a tough habit to break later.

LESSON 6: HOW TO READ TABLATURE

Tablature (or TAB for short) is a system of writing music for fretted instruments that shows exactly which string to play, on which fret, and with which finger. There are five lines in banjo TAB, which represent the five strings on your banjo. The top line is the *1st string*, which is the one closest to the floor when you are holding your banjo in playing position. In the example below, the "0" on the third line means to play the 3rd string open (not fretted). The "T" underneath means to pick it with the thumb of the right hand. The next note is the 1st string played at the 2nd fret and picked with the middle finger.

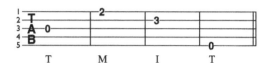

Standard Music Notation
Because notes overlap so closely on the banjo, TAB is used much more frequently than standard music notation. If you can already read music, great! A lot of that knowledge will be helpful, but if not, don't worry. We'll explain it all as we move through the book.

LESSON 7: TIME

MEASURES AND BEATS

The *beat* is the steady, rhythmic pulse of music, which we use to measure musical time. It's where you'd tap your foot or clap your hands. Written music and TAB are organized into *measures,* also called *bars,* and each measure contains an equal number of beats. *Bar lines* are the vertical lines that separate measures as shown in the example below.

NOTE VALUES

Every note has a specific duration, or *value.* In most music, a *whole note* is the longest note value, usually lasting four beats, or a whole measure. In TAB, there is no *stem* (see the example below). If you understand fractions, understanding the other note values is easy; just think them as being fractions of the whole note. A *half note* is half the value of a whole note, or two beats. In TAB, the number in a half note is circled and there is a stem. A *quarter note,* with a stem and no circle, is half the value of a half note, or a quarter of a whole note, and is one beat. An *eighth note* is half the value of a quarter note, or an eighth of a whole note, and has a stem and a *beam.* There are of course other note values, but we'll get to them later.

TIME SIGNATURES

The *time signature* tells you how many beats are in each measure and which kind of note will be counted as one beat. In the example below, the time signature is $\frac{4}{4}$. The top number indicates that each measure will contain four beats, and the bottom number indicates that a quarter note will equal one beat. The $\frac{4}{4}$ time signature is so frequently used that we also call it *common time.*

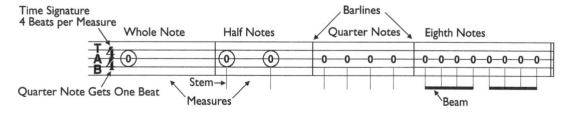

THE MUSICAL ALPHABET

The musical alphabet goes from A to G and then repeats. These notes—A, B, C, D, E, F, and G—are called the *natural notes*. As we move forward through the alphabet (from A to G), the pitches of the notes become higher. As we move backward through the alphabet (from G down to A), the pitches become lower. Between some of the natural notes (but not all) are *chromatic notes*, or *sharps* (in standard music notation, this is signified by the *sharp sign* ♯) and *flats* (signified by the *flat sign* ♭). It's easiest to explain this by showing it on a piano keyboard where (pardon the pun) it's all right here in black and white:

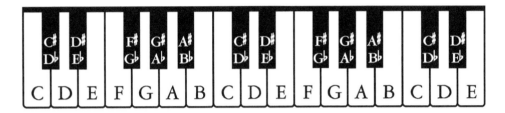

The white keys on the piano keyboard are the natural notes, and the black keys between them are the chromatic notes (sharps and flats). These can also be *enharmonic,* or *enharmonic equivalents,* which means that each chromatic note can be called by two names. For example, A♯ and B♭ are enharmonic equivalents; they are the same pitch but can be called by either name. Notice there is no sharp or flat (no black key) between B and C or between E and F.

HALF STEPS AND WHOLE STEPS

If you were to move from A to B on the piano keyboard, skipping over the note in between (A♯ or B♭), you will have moved a *whole step*. Moving from A to A♯ (or B♭) is a movement of a *half step*. On the banjo, moving a distance of two frets is a whole step, and moving the distance of one fret is a half step. As you go through the musical alphabet, all natural notes have whole steps between them, except B to C and E to F, which are half steps.

Combining this concept with your knowledge of the names of the notes of the open strings will enable you to find any note on the banjo fretboard! For example, the 3rd string open is tuned to a G. Fret the 3rd string at the 1st fret (a half step above the open string) and you'll get G♯ or A♭. Fret the 3rd string at the 2nd fret (a whole step above the open string) and you'll get an A.

The chart below shows the names of the notes on the banjo fretboard:

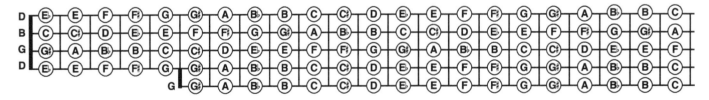

If this seems like a lot to memorize, don't worry, you don't have to! It can all be summarized in three easy steps:

1. The musical alphabet goes from A to G with chromatic notes in between and then starts over.
2. All natural notes have whole steps between them, except for B to C and E to F, which are half steps.
3. Moving a distance of one fret is a half step and two frets is a whole step.

If no ♯ or ♭ sign is present, then the note is a natural note. However, sometimes it's necessary to specify the identity of a natural note. In these cases, a *natural sign* ♮ is used. It's great to learn to read standard music notation and be familiar with all of the rules of writing chromatic notes, but those skills will not be required for this method.

We'll start with a couple of well-known melodies that are easy to play. Read the TAB to play the tunes, but be sure to listen to and watch the accompanying audio and video as you move along. Pay close attention to your timing and try to play the melody just like you would sing it, with one note per syllable. Remember, you're not just playing notes here—you're playing music!

YANKEE DOODLE

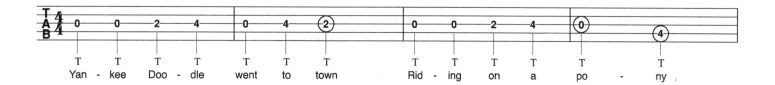

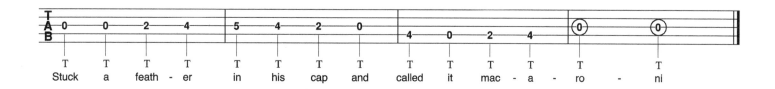

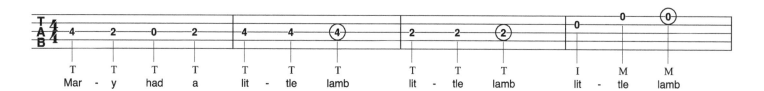

MARY HAD A LITTLE LAMB

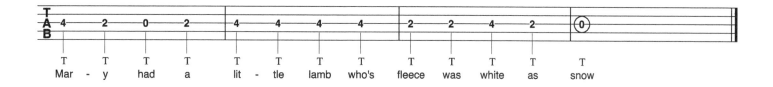

ODE TO JOY

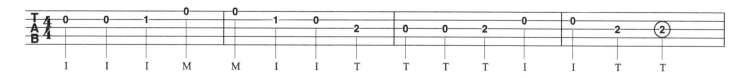

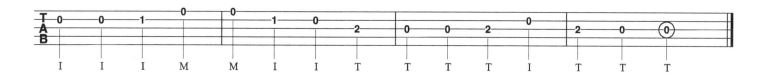

LESSON 10: FILL-IN NOTES

Fill-in notes are notes used to fill the spaces between the melody notes. You probably noticed that the songs we've played so far don't sound much like real banjo playing. Fill-in notes will help create that signature sound.

THE 5TH–1ST FILL-IN

As the name implies, the *5th–1st fill-in* is done by playing the 5th string and then the 1st string as eighth notes, creating a *syncopation*. Syncopation is a shift of the emphasis to an unexpected place, such as from the first beat to the second, or from the first eighth note in a beat to the second. Inserting a 5th–1st fill-in in eighth notes is one way to accomplish this.

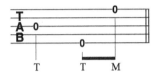

Instead of the straight 1–2–3–4 rhythm of quarter notes, the 5th–1st fill-in will give it a rhythm of 1–2&–3–4&. Try to count that rhythm aloud when you play the next example.

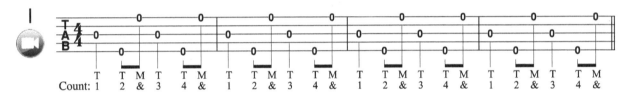

THE PINCH

A *pinch* is a technique where you play two strings together, one with the thumb and the other with I or M. The most common pinch is one that we use as a fill-in, also on the 5th and 1st strings. In TAB it looks like this:

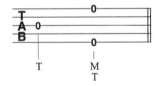

Let's try alternating pinches with 5th–1st fill-ins.

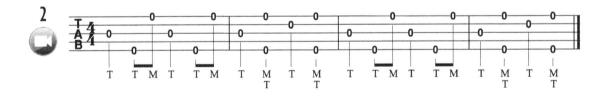

> Note that while most banjo music is usually written in $\frac{4}{4}$ time with eighth notes, implying four beats with eight eighth notes per measure, we're typically feeling only two beats per measure with four eighth notes in each beat when we get it worked up to speed. Most of the music in this method can be felt this way.

Now let's put these fill-ins to work in a couple of songs. Remember to try to keep the melody even and clear, just like you would sing it, and use the fill-ins to add a bit of syncopation.

SKIP TO MY LOU

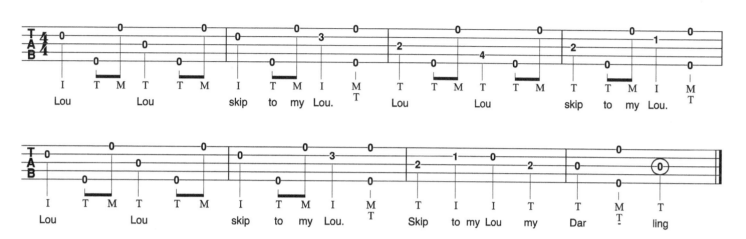

GO TELL AUNT RHODY (NO. 1)

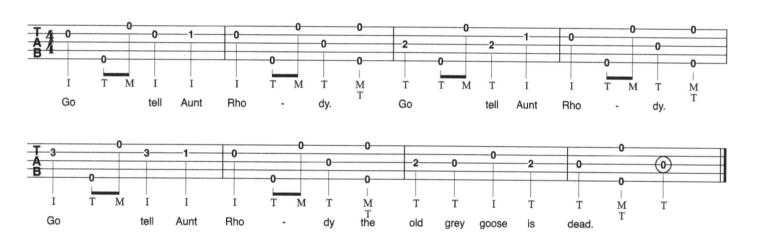

GRANDFATHER'S CLOCK

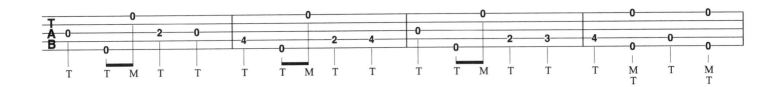

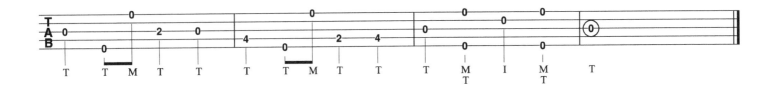

Learning Songs by Ear

To learn a song by ear means to learn it just by hearing it, or by remembering it, and then figuring it out on your own (without written music or without anyone showing you). Although it may seem like magic when a musician learns songs instantly, just by hearing them, it's not. It's a skill that can be developed, and you can start doing it now!

So far, the songs in this book were chosen because they're easy to play and (hopefully) very familiar. Once you're comfortable with playing the tunes in this chapter, try picking some out on your own. Start with something easy: Think about the bugle calls used by the military, "Reveille" and "Taps." Both can be played on just the open strings of the banjo (no fretted notes). Then try figuring out other simple tunes you know. Folk songs, camp songs, church hymns, and even TV show themes and pop tunes are all fair game. It is always a little bit of a trial-and-error process, but the more experienced you get, the fewer errors you'll make. Being able to learn songs by ear will come in very handy once you start playing with other people.

CHAPTER 2
Chords

A *chord* is three or more notes played together. Chords can be used to accompany yourself singing or to accompany other singers or musicians. The first chords we'll learn are *open chords*, which are chords that use a combination of open and fretted strings. As mentioned earlier, you're playing an open G chord when you play all the open strings on your banjo.

CHORD DIAGRAM

Chords are often shown with a *chord diagram*, which is a snapshot of the banjo fretboard, showing the strings, frets, and finger placement needed to play a particular chord. You'll notice that the 5th string is not usually included in banjo chord diagrams; the banjo 5th string is not usually fretted or played for chords.

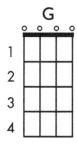
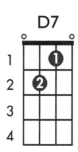
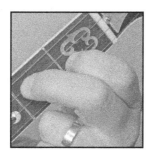

Fretting the open D7 chord.

PLAYING CHORDS

When you play the D7 chord, hold the strings down with just the fingertips and make sure your fingers are only touching the strings you intend to play. If your fretting-hand fingernails are so long that they're hitting the fretboard, you may need to trim them. Try picking the strings one at a time as you fret the chord, adjusting your finger positions until each note is clear and not muffled.

STRUMMING THE BANJO

The 5-string banjo is more often picked than strummed (don't worry, we'll get back to picking soon). Strumming is a great way to practice changing chords. Strum down toward the floor with either your thumb or the fingernail of your index finger (you won't need your fingerpicks for this). Position your strumming finger on the 4th string and then move down quickly, hitting all of the top four strings at once.

When strumming the banjo, it's usually best to avoid playing the 5th string. The 5th string sounds good for some chords but not so good in others. Since it's not possible to fret the 5th string when you play open chords, the best option is to simply avoid it.

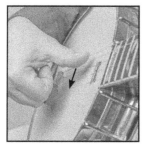
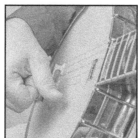

Strumming with the right-hand thumb.   *Strumming with the right-hand index finger.*

READING A CHORD CHART

A *chord chart* shows you which chords to play, when to change them, and when to strum. The slashes represent the beats in each measure. We'll start with a simple four-beat, quarter-note rhythm with an open G chord. Count out the rhythm, 1–2–3–4, as you strum down on the strings, and keep the rhythm steady.

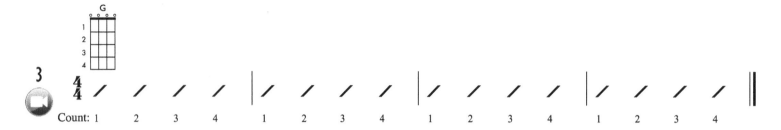

Now let's try it with the two chords we know so far, G and D7. Keep the pace slow so that you can play without stopping or slowing down when switching between chords.

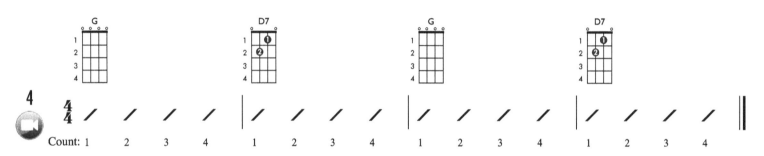

Chord Changing Tip

Once you're comfortable with the D7 chord, try lifting your fingers just barely off the strings while still holding them in the chord shape. Then put both fingers back down at the same time instead of one at a time. Practicing this way will help you retain the chord shape in your muscle memory, which will help you change chords faster. If your fingers are a little tender, repeated practice will help you develop calluses to toughen your fingers up. The key is to practice every day. More tips about practicing can be found in the Appendix section of this book (page 92).

LESSON 2: TWO-CHORD SONGS

Now that you know two chords (G and D7), there are dozens of songs that you can play! Follow the chord charts for "Tom Dooley" and "Handsome Molly" and sing along. Both songs feature *pickup notes*, which are notes that occur before the first full measure.

Strum along with "Tom Dooley." Strum when you see the slash marks, and change chords as indicated. Keep the rhythm steady, and don't slow down to change chords. Notice there's a new time signature for this song, $\frac{2}{4}$. So far, we've been playing in $\frac{4}{4}$ time, which means there are four quarter notes per measure. In $\frac{2}{4}$, there are two quarter notes per measure.

TOM DOOLEY

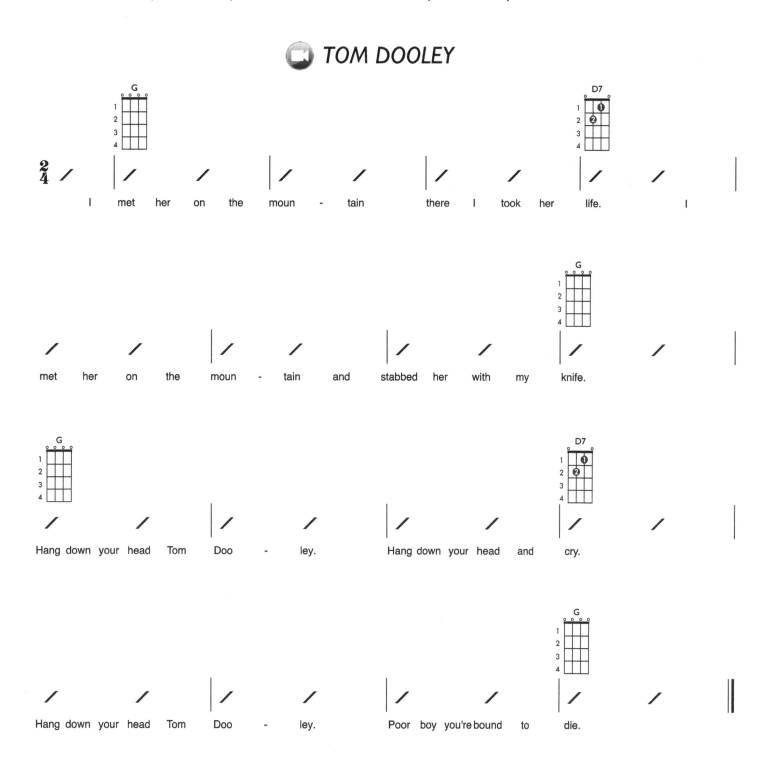

HANDSOME MOLLY

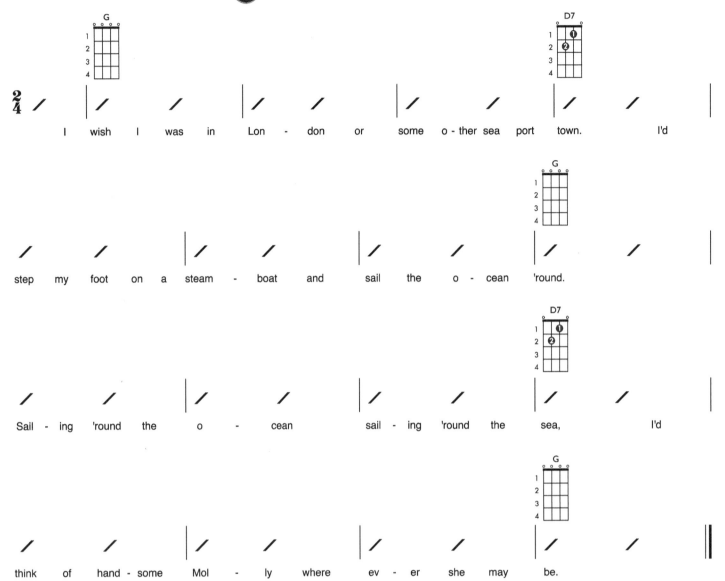

Once you are comfortable, try playing the songs we've learned so far from memory without looking at the book and anticipate when chord changes happen. Then, try singing those songs without the banjo and see if you can hear when the changes should happen. Once you can do this, there are many other songs you can play with just G and D7, including:

John Henry	Buffalo Gals	I'm Going Back to Old Kentucky
Katy Daley	Pretty Polly	Hot Corn, Cold Corn
Little Birdie	Shady Grove	Ashes of Love
Stay All Night	Jambalaya	Take Me Back to Tulsa

The next chord in open position is the C chord.

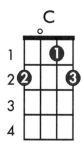
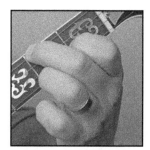

Fretting the open C chord.

Now let's try switching from G to C. Keep the beat even and strum each chord four times.

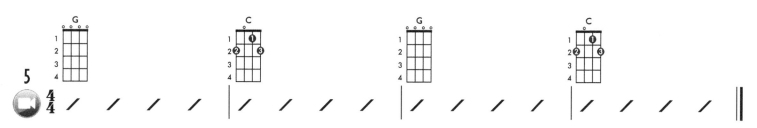

Next we'll play all three chords we know: G, C, and D7. Notice that your 1st finger stays in the same place for both the C and the D7 chords.

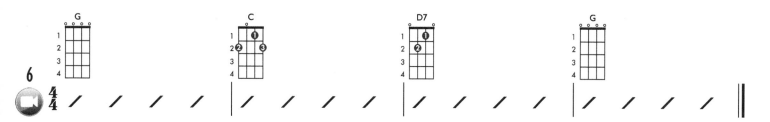

Three Chords and the Truth
"Three chords and the truth" is what country songwriter Harlan Howard said was the key to a great country song. It turns out, it's also the key to a great bluegrass song, rock song, blues song, and many others. Armed with just the G, C, and D7 chords, there are hundreds, and perhaps thousands, of songs you can play. Later, we'll discuss the theory behind these three chords and how to move into other keys, but for now, "three chords and the truth" expresses how important these three chords—and being able to change between them—are to your banjo-playing future!

Let's put our three chords, G, C, and D7, to use to play some familiar songs.

GOOD OL' MOUNTAIN DEW (NO. 1)

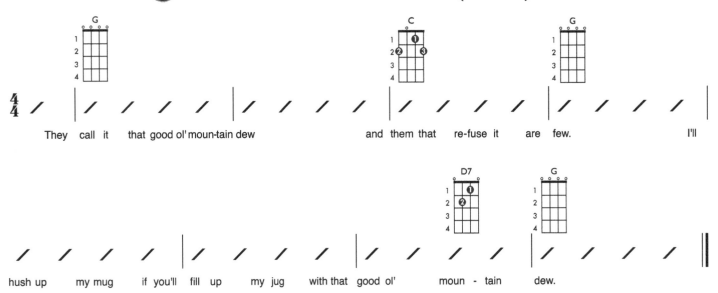

They call it that good ol' moun-tain dew   and them that re-fuse it are few.   I'll

hush up   my mug   if you'll fill up   my jug   with that good ol'   moun - tain   dew.

WORRIED MAN BLUES

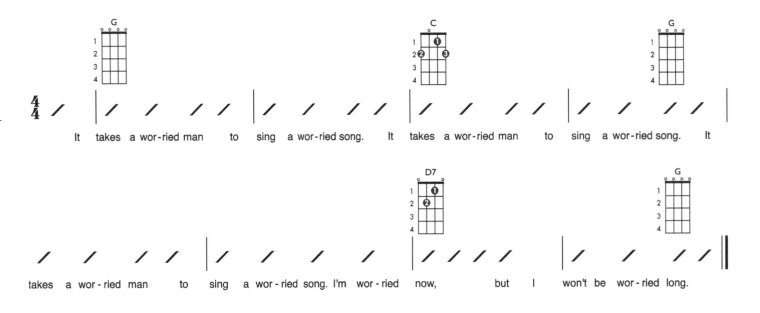

It takes a wor-ried man to sing a wor-ried song.   It takes a wor-ried man   to sing a wor-ried song.   It

takes a wor-ried man   to sing a wor-ried song. I'm wor-ried   now,   but I   won't be wor-ried long.

CHAPTER 3

Rolls

The fingerpicking patterns used in banjo playing are known as *rolls*. Bluegrass-style banjo is made up of a combination of rolls, chords, and a few other techniques—but at the heart of it are banjo rolls.

LESSON 1: BASIC ROLLS

THE FORWARD ROLL

The *forward roll* is played by picking with the T, I, and M fingers in that specific order. It can be played on different combinations of strings and can start with any finger, but it is always in the T–I–M order.

Here are three examples of different forward-roll patterns:

Right-Hand Finger Review		
T	=	Thumb
I	=	Index finger
M	=	Middle finger

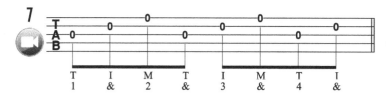

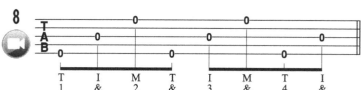

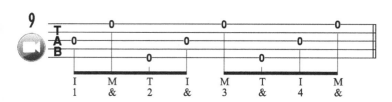

As you can see in the examples above, the forward roll is played in eighth notes (eight notes per measure). Since eight can't be evenly divided by three (there are eight notes per measure but only three notes in a forward roll), there's one note left off the end of the measure, which makes it much easier to hear where a new measure begins when you are repeating these patterns.

Try playing the forward-roll pattern below, which does not leave off the last note in the roll. You'll notice that each measure starts on a different note.

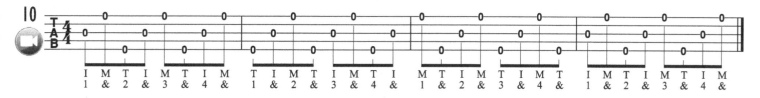

Now try the following, where the first roll in each measure has the T stroke left off.

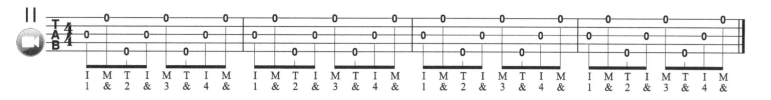

Let's try a couple of tunes using forward rolls.

GO TELL AUNT RHODY (NO. 2)

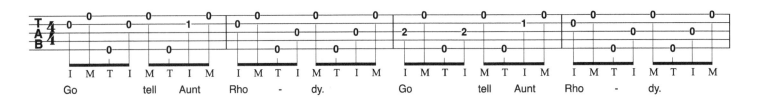

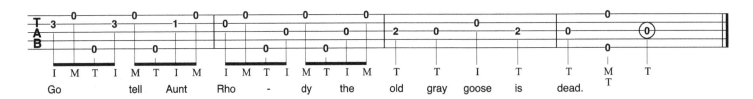

In "Boil Them Cabbage Down," you'll combine the forward roll with the open G, C, and D7 chords to play the melody. Play it slowly so that you can make the chord changes without stopping the roll, and keep the rhythm as even as possible. Once you can make the chord changes faster, you can try speeding up the roll. Also notice that applying the roll to the melody causes a slight syncopation. This is a very common sound in banjo playing.

BOIL THEM CABBAGE DOWN (NO. 1)

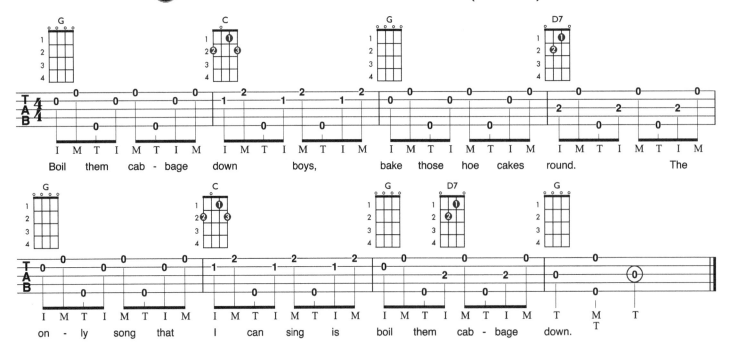

THE FOGGY MOUNTAIN ROLL

The *Foggy Mountain roll* is a variation of the forward roll. It gets its name from the song "Foggy Mountain Breakdown," and it's the roll played at the beginning of that song. Note that the third note in each measure below is played with the thumb (T) on the 2nd string. While it may appear easier to use your index finger (I), once you get going a little faster, it's actually easier and a little more powerful with the thumb.

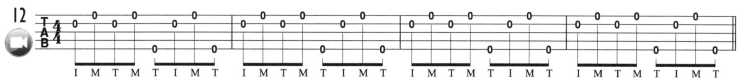

Now let's put the Foggy Mountain roll through its paces by playing it with the G, C, and D7 chords.

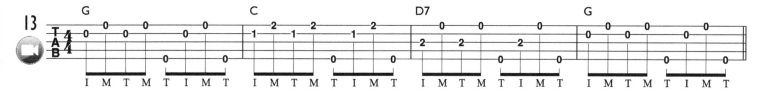

THE BACKWARD ROLL

The *backward roll* is just what it sounds like: it's the opposite of the forward roll. Instead of T–I–M, your right hand will be moving in the direction of M–I–T. Here are a couple of examples:

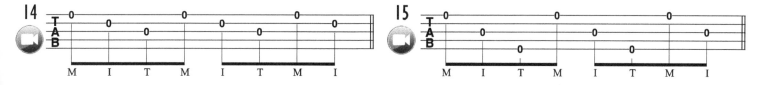

Let's extend Ex. 15 to help us get the backward roll under our fingers:

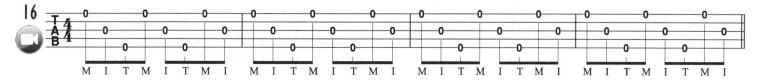

Practicing Rolls
Practice playing all of these rolls until you have them memorized, and then practice them some more! Playing rolls every day will not only increase your accuracy with striking the correct strings, but it will also help improve your timing. Try to keep the notes evenly spaced, like the ticking of a stopwatch. Practicing with a *metronome* (an adjustable device that provides a click to play with) can help. To learn more about metronomes, check out the Appendix (page 92).

THE FORWARD-REVERSE ROLL

As its name implies, the *forward-reverse roll* starts as a forward roll and then reverses halfway through. Following are a few variations of the forward-reverse roll.

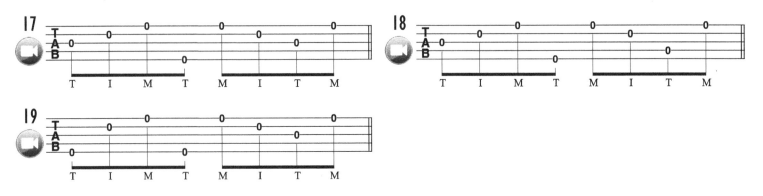

Ex. 18 is a good one to practice because it uses all five strings. Let's repeat that one for a while:

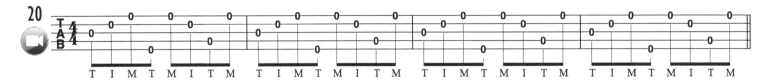

By combining the forward-reverse roll with the G, C, and D7 chords, the melody to "Worried Man Blues" comes out rather nicely.

WORRIED MAN BLUES (NO. 1)

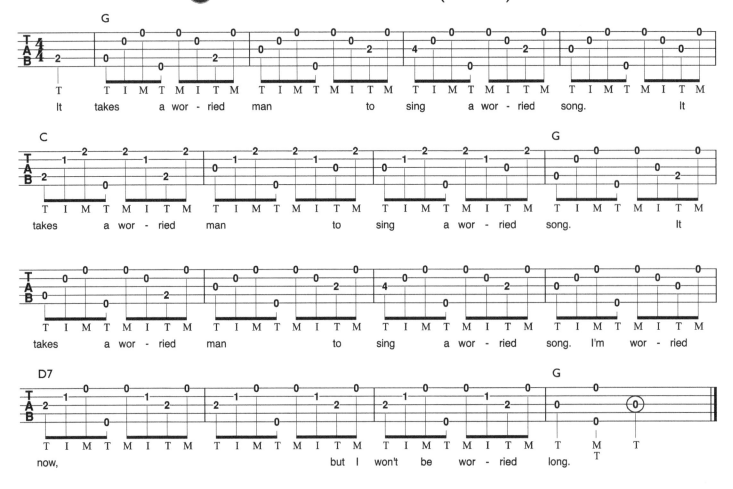

THE ALTERNATING ROLL

The *alternating roll* makes use of all five strings and has an easily recognizable *alternating bass-note pattern* where the lowest notes in the chord repeat back and forth—hence the name. The bass notes are the lowest-sounding notes. Get to know this one well.

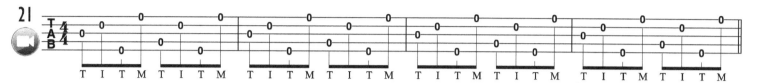

Since it uses all five strings, changing chords with the alternating roll is a great way to tell if you are fingering the chords cleanly.

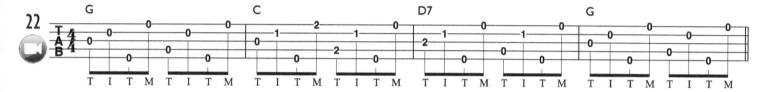

LESSON 2: COMBINING ROLLS

Very few songs are played with only one roll. By using the rolls in different combinations, more melodic and rhythmic variations can be achieved.

Try practicing one roll for two bars, then switch to another for two bars, and then to another. You should be able to switch from one roll to another without any interruption in the rhythm. Below are a few combinations to try.

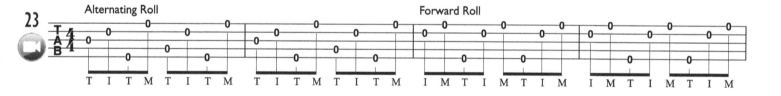

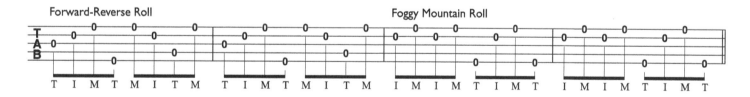

Try the rolls in different combinations once you've played through Ex. 23. When you have them memorized well enough, you will be able to switch between them without slowing down or stopping.

This arrangement of "Worried Man Blues" uses a combination of forward-reverse and forward rolls. Compare it to the arrangement on page 26, which used only the forward-reverse roll. Varying the rolls makes the song sound less repetitious.

WORRIED MAN BLUES (NO. 2)

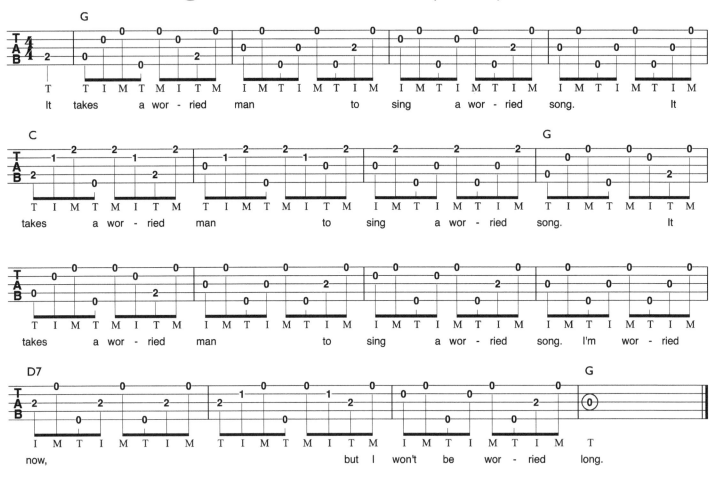

LESSON 3: COMBINING ROLLS AND FILL-INS

Now we'll combine the rolls we learned in this chapter with some of the fill-ins from Chapter 1.

Try this exercise. It's a forward-reverse roll with repeated pinches.

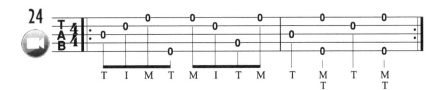

This one combines the alternating roll with the 5th–1st fill-in. (They're almost the same!)

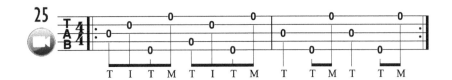

The Repeat Sign

Repeat signs indicate a section of music should be repeated.

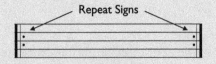

Repeat Signs

When you see the right-facing opening repeat sign, be on the lookout as the left-facing closing one will follow. When you see the closing sign, go back to the opening sign to play the section between the signs again. Repeat signs are a shortcut for music notation, so that we don't have to rewrite sections of identical music.

This arrangement of "Camptown Races" incorporates all of the techniques you've learned so far. It starts with a simple statement of the melody, then uses fill-ins and rolls. Although the chords are included for this song, you may notice a few places where the TAB does not require you to fret the chord. The melody of a song sometimes uses notes that are not part of the chord. The chord changes are there for accompaniment purposes only. Imagine two half-note slash rhythm marks per measure, and you can strum the chords to this song just as you did with the songs in Chapter 2.

CAMPTOWN RACES

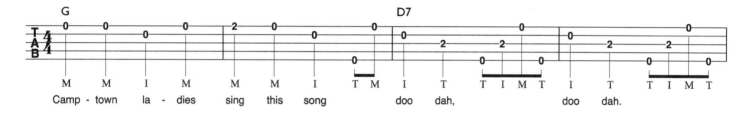

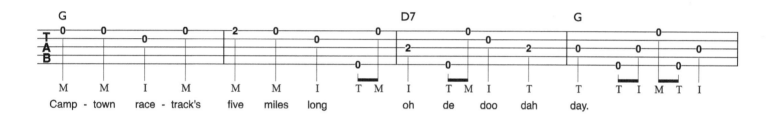

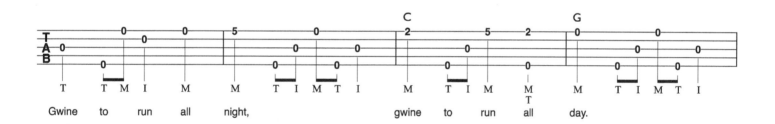

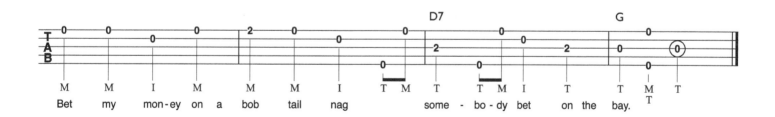

In this arrangement of "Red River Valley," we will be combining two styles of playing. The first is incorporating the melody into rolls, as we did in "Worried Man Blues," and the second is playing melody notes with fill-ins, as we just did in "Camptown Races." The lyrics to the song are printed under the melody notes to help you identify where you are in the song. Try singing along (either out loud or inside your head) to keep the melody clear and strong.

RED RIVER VALLEY

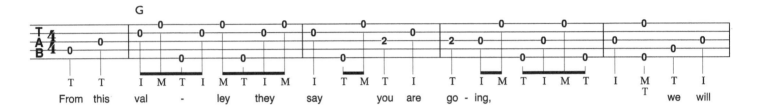

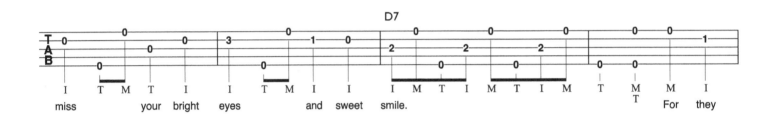

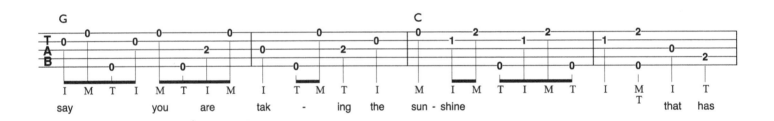

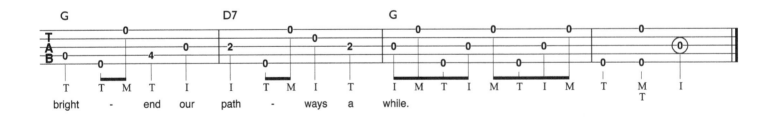

CHAPTER 4

Licks and Left-Hand Techniques

A *lick* is a short musical phrase that can be used to build a large idea or be part of an improvised a solo. Licks are to a tune as words are to a story. In this chapter, you will learn some essential left-hand techniques, such as *slides*, *pull-offs* and *hammer-ons*, and we'll use them to form some useful licks that will turn into the building blocks of solos.

LESSON 1: SLIDES

To perform a *slide,* play a fretted note and then, while still holding the string down on the fretboard, slide your finger along the string to a higher fret (slides rarely go to a lower fret). A slide can cover a distance of one or several frets. Slides are indicated in TAB by a slur ⌒ and a diagonal line between the two fret numbers and is signified by an SL mark.

Try the following examples of one-, two-, and three-fret slides. Play the first note, then move your left hand quickly so that the second note is heard before the string stops ringing.

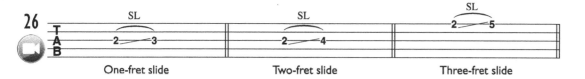

One-fret slide   Two-fret slide   Three-fret slide

Often, when slides are incorporated into licks, the second note of the slide is meant to sound simultaneously with a note played on another string. In this next example, play the 3rd string at the 2nd fret with T, and then as you slide to the 3rd fret on that string, play the open 2nd string with I at the same time. The slur will help you see which notes to slide.

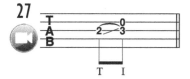

Ex. 28 gives you an opportunity to practice the previous concept a few times in a row until it becomes smooth, where you hear just two eighth notes in each slide, not three.

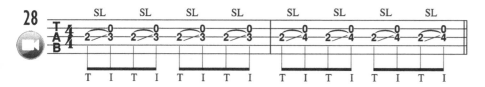

Now try this one. You'll be doing the same slide, but following it up by playing the 1st string with M.

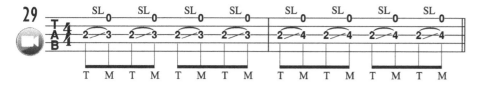

Now we'll combine the slide with an alternating roll to create a slide lick.

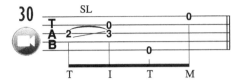

Try to keep the second note of the slide from sounding before the open 2nd string is played.

Next we'll string a few slide licks together.

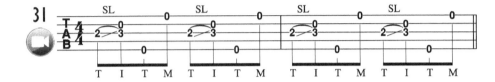

Here's the same slide from Ex. 31 but with a forward-reverse roll.

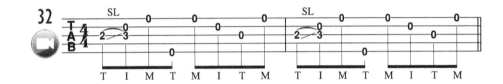

So far, we've been concentrating on slides on the 3rd string. Slides can be played on any string, but sliding on the 3rd string is integral to playing bluegrass-style banjo. We'll get to more slides later, but in the meantime, let's put the 3rd-string slide into action right away in a familiar tune.

Use the slide along with a forward-reverse roll, a forward roll, and some fill-ins to help state the melody to "Boil Them Cabbage Down."

BOIL THEM CABBAGE DOWN (NO. 2)

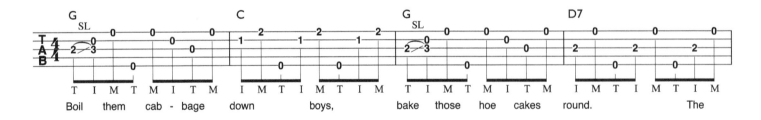

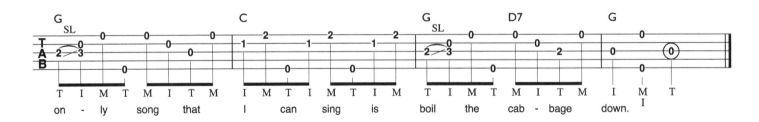

A *hammer-on* is played by picking a string and then, while the note is still ringing, fretting the string without picking to produce a second, higher note. The key is to fret the string quickly and just forcefully enough (like a hammer) to produce a second note. A hammer-on can be played on an open string, too. Pick the open string, then hammer-on to any fret on the string. In TAB, a hammer-on is indicated with a slur ⌒ and the letter H.

Try the following hammer-on. Play the 1st string open and then using the 2nd finger of your fretting hand, fret the 2nd fret in a quick, hammer-like motion.

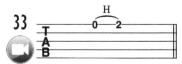

Now try a hammer-on from a fretted note. Fret the 2nd fret of the 1st string with your 1st finger. Now pick the string and hammer-on to the 3rd fret with your 2nd finger to produce the second note.

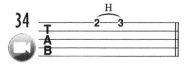

Following is an exercise that has four hammer-ons in a row. Play evenly, giving each picked note and each hammered-on note the same time value. Count them as 1&–2&–3&–4&.

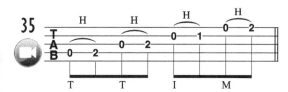

Hammer-ons can be combined with picked notes to play melodies. This is especially true in old-time banjo styles (which we'll explore more in Chapter 9). Following is a tune that uses hammer-ons to play a catchy, traditional-sounding melody.

🎦 HAMMERVILLE

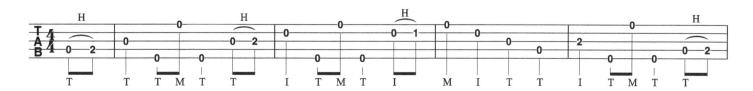

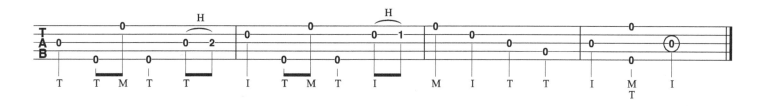

Now let's try a hammer-on with a second note played simultaneously, like we did with the slide. Play the 4th string open, then hammer on to the 2nd fret with your 2nd finger while you play the 2nd string with I. The 2nd-finger note and open 2nd string should sound simultaneously.

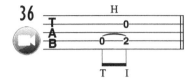

Practice the following example slowly at first. Play the the open 4th string and let it ring for a second or two, then hammer on with your left hand and pick with your right hand at the same time. Once you can do this easily, try to speed it up a little, repeating it a few times.

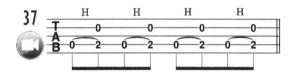

Try this hammer-on combined with the forward roll. This is the first lick in the song "Cumberland Gap." Like the slide lick, the sound of the hammered note should happen simultaneously with the note on the open 2nd string. Play the open 4th string and then play the 2nd string at the same time as the hammer-on.

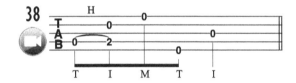

The song "Cumberland Gap" uses the hammer-on lick we just learned, a forward-reverse roll with a slide, and a couple of pinches. Keep an eye on the eighth notes and quarter notes. The rhythm of measures 1, 2, and 4 are the same. (Since the first four measures are repeated, we'll see the same rhythm in measures 5, 6, and 8 as well.)

CUMBERLAND GAP

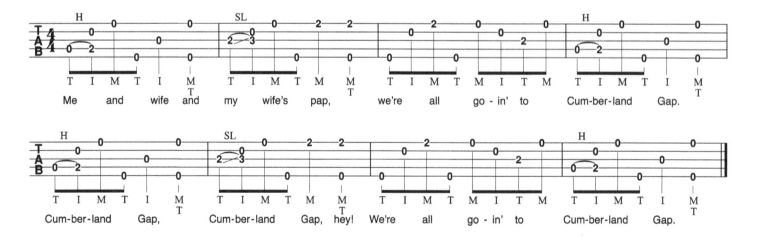

The *pull-off* can be thought of as the opposite of the hammer-on. It's played by picking a note on a fretted string and then pulling your finger off the string to sound a second, lower note. A pull-off can be played from a fretted note to an open string, or from a fretted note to another fretted note on a lower fret. Pull-offs are indicated in TAB with a slur ⌒ and the letter P.

Try a pull-off to an open string. Play the 1st string at the 2nd fret and then pull your left-hand finger off of the string. Instead of lifting your finger straight up, pull it slightly downward, toward the floor. You'll actually be picking the string with your left hand.

39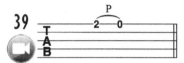

Now try a pull-off to a fretted note. Place your 2nd finger on the 1st string, 3rd fret and your 1st finger on the 2nd fret of the same string. Play the 3rd-fret note, then pull your 2nd finger off the string with your 1st finger in place. You should now hear the 2nd-fret note.

40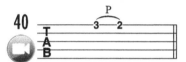

To play an open-string pull-off on the 4th string, you may find it easier to push the finger up instead of pulling down towards the floor. This will help keep you from hitting other strings with your left hand.

41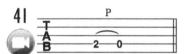

Playing a pull-off on the 2nd or 3rd string is a little trickier. Avoid hitting any other strings with your finger after the pull-off. Try pulling down (toward the floor) but a little bit up, too, to avoid bumping the adjacent string. Also experiment with pushing up toward the 4th string to see which way works best for you.

42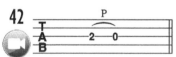

One more: This is a pull-off from the 3rd fret to the 2nd fret on the 3rd string. It's pretty much the same as Ex. 40, but it may be trickier to keep from hitting other strings with this one. It'll take a little practice, but it will come.

43

Like the hammer-on, the pull-off can be sounded alone or with a simultaneous note. Let's try doing some pull-offs in time as eighth notes. We'll start with the 1st string, 2nd fret.

44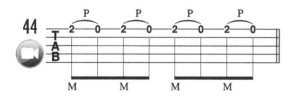

Try the same thing at the 4th fret. **45**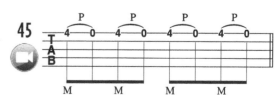

Try the following exercise by playing the fretted notes and then pulling off to the open strings, one at a time. This is the opposite of the hammer-on exercise in the last section.

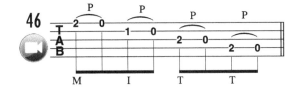

Here's a little tune using some pull-offs and 5th–1st fill-ins. Keep the timing of the pull-offs as eighth notes and this should be an easy one to "pull off."

PULL-OFF TOWNE

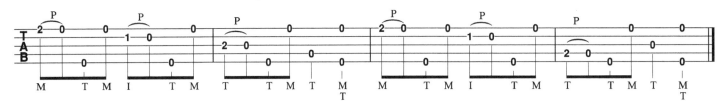

Play the next example by picking the 3rd string at the 2nd fret and then pulling off to the open string while picking the 1st string with M at the same time. As in the slide and hammer-on exercises, do this very slowly at first and don't speed up until you can execute the technique comfortably.

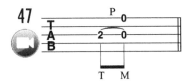

This time, use I to pick the 2nd string with the pull-off note.

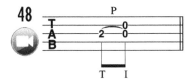

Now let's put these pull-offs to use by combining them with rolls to create some licks.

Just like the slide and hammer-on licks, try to play the pull-off simultaneously with the open 2nd string.

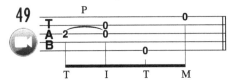

Let's string a couple of these together and practice them in rhythm. The timing is the same as the alternating roll.

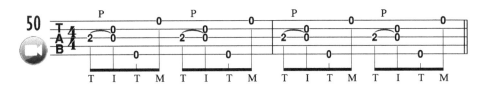

Are Your Fingers Hurting Yet?
If you've never played a string instrument before, your fingertips are likely to be getting a bit tender by now. Also, the added movement of changing chords, and now all these slides, hammer-ons and pull-offs, require you to move your fingers in ways you're probably not accustomed to. This is another reason to practice every day. When you skip a day or two of practice, the calluses you've been developing get soft and you lose some of the muscle memory in your fingers. Practice every day and, before long, you won't believe how easy these things have become. Keep at it! *Every day!* It'll be worth it.

LESSON 4: COMBINING SLIDES, HAMMER-ONS, AND PULL-OFFS

Here's where the real fun starts! Let's combine slides, pull-offs, and hammer-ons to create some real banjo solos. Ready?

We'll start by combining the slide, pull-off, and hammer-on licks we learned in the previous lessons.

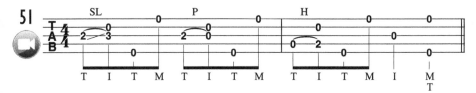

If this sounds familiar, it's because these are the last few licks in the song "Cripple Creek," which you'll be learning next. The second part of "Cripple Creek" begins with three slide licks, the open 4th string, and a pinch, which is followed up by the combination we just learned above. Try this:

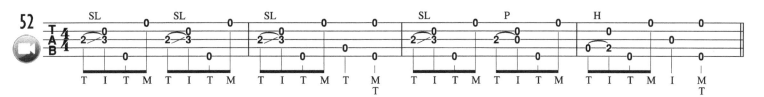

The next lick we need for "Cripple Creek" is a big one. It's a slide from the 2nd fret to the 5th fret on the 1st string. Start by playing a pinch of the 1st and 5th strings together while fretting the 2nd fret of the 1st string. Then, slide the note from the 2nd fret all the way to the 5th fret. Don't go too fast, both notes are eighth notes. And the second note is not picked; it's the slide note.

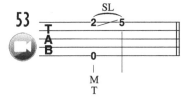

The first note of the slide in the first part of "Cripple Creek" is a pickup note. The pinch comes on beat 4, and the slide note lands on beat 1 of the first measure. Count 1, 2, 3, then play the pinch on 4, and slide so that you reach the 5th fret on beat 1 of the second measure.

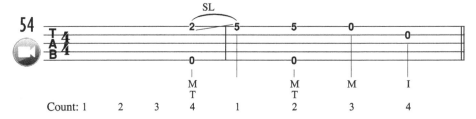

Let's take a look at the rest of the first part of "Cripple Creek," including how the beats are counted:

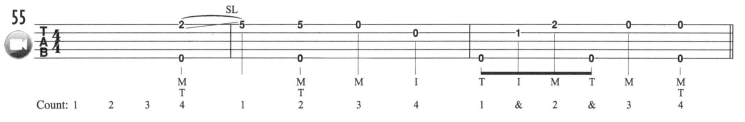

Now let's put together all the sections you've learned to play "Cripple Creek."

CRIPPLE CREEK

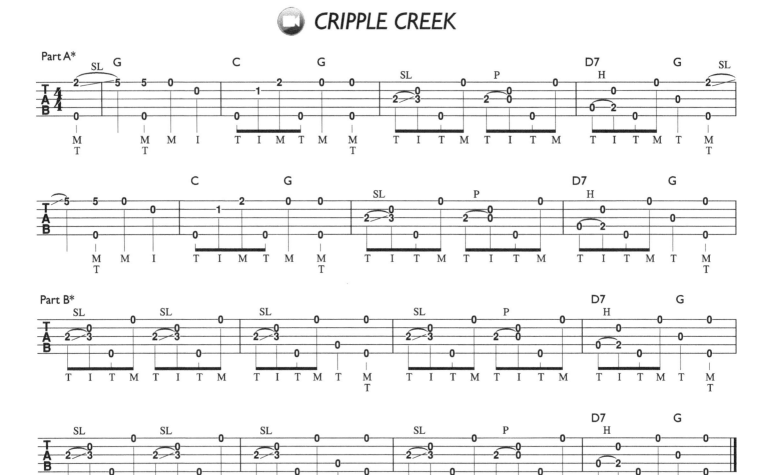

> *** Verse and Chorus vs. Part A and Part B**
> "Cripple Creek" is a song with lyrics, but it is much more commonly played as an instrumental. Most bluegrass, country, blues, and folk songs have several *verses* and then a repeated *chorus*. A verse is the part of a song that tells the story and changes with each repetition. The chorus is the repeated refrain of the song and is generally the same each time. Sometimes the verse and chorus have the same melody and chords, but often they do not. Instrumental songs are like this, too, except that instead of verse and chorus, they are usually referred to as the *Part A* and *Part B*. (Note: the "A" and "B" have nothing to do with the chords, A and B!)

"Waterbound" uses several of the techniques we've learned so far. Pay attention to the note on the 2nd fret right after the slide in measure 2 as it may be tricky. Also keep an eye on the slides in measures 1 and 6. These slides are the same but their rolls differ.

WATERBOUND

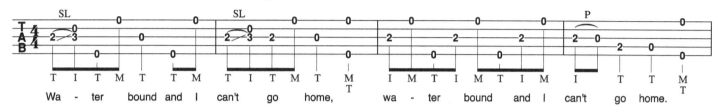

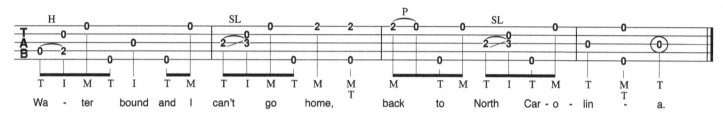

Here are a few more essential licks to add to your banjo vocabulary.

THE FOGGY MOUNTAIN LICK

By adding a hammer-on to the 2nd string, you can play one of the most useful and recognizable licks in the banjo repertoire.

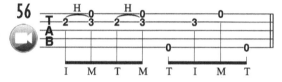

This next lick is often played as an intro (see page 44 for more on intros) to banjo tunes and is usually repeated two or three times in a row. Remember to use your thumb on the 2nd string where indicated.

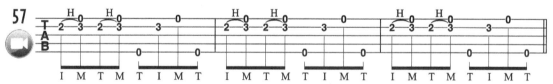

This pull-off lick often follows the Foggy Mountain lick. It's a forward roll starting on the 5th string. Play it slowly and when you get to the 3rd string, 3rd fret, pick that note and then play the pull-off and 1st-string note at the same time.

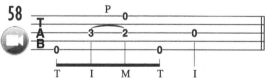

The next pull-off lick uses the same forward roll as the last four notes of the Foggy Mountain roll. Just move your 1st finger to the 3rd string and play the pull-off instead of the open string.

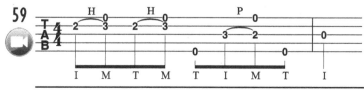

Let's try the pull-off lick combined with three measures of the Foggy Mountain lick.

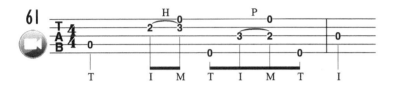

Here's another variation, this time modified to be an ending lick.

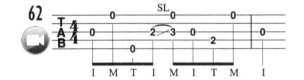

FILL-IN LICKS AND TAG LICKS

When arranging a banjo solo around the melody of a song, there may sometimes be a bar or two at the end of a line where the melody pauses but the rhythm continues. Look back to the arrangement of "Red River Valley" on page 30. The next-to-last measure contains a forward-reverse roll that is only there to keep the time. Fill-in licks are used to fill in spaces between melodic passages, while *tag licks* are used to end a phrase. Often they can be very similar (or even exactly the same), and the difference in name only applies to the context in which they are used.

The following is one of the most all-purpose fill-in licks. Try using this lick in "Red River Valley" in place of the forward roll in the last line. It adds a nice finishing touch to the tune.

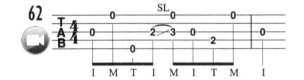

Or you could play this variation instead:

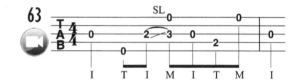

The variation is exactly the same as Ex. 62 but without the second note. The missing note gives it a different rhythmic feel.

"Train 45" is a popular banjo tune that uses the Foggy Mountain lick, the fill-in tag lick, and a couple of pinches. Although the tune is fairly easy, it's often played very fast. Be careful and watch your speed! Make sure you can play it clearly, cleanly, and evenly at a slow speed before trying to crank it up.

 *TRAIN 45*

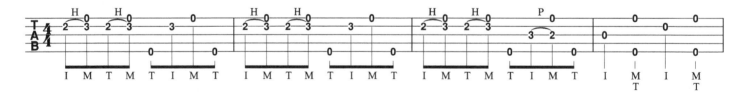

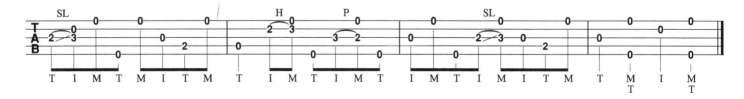

SLIDE PULL-OFF COMBO

This lick uses a forward-reverse roll in combination with a slide and a pull-off. It is useful for playing the melody but also works well as a fill-in lick

Use the 2nd finger of your left hand to slide up to the 3rd fret, and then keep it there until you get to the pull-off.

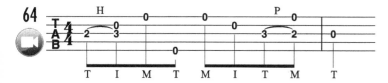

This song uses the slide/pull-off combo to set the melody and also features a couple of excellent examples of fill-in and tag licks.

GOOD OL' MOUNTAIN DEW (NO. 2)

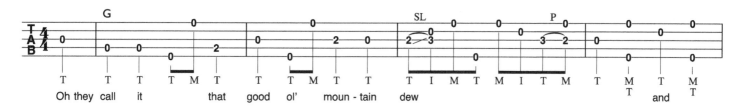

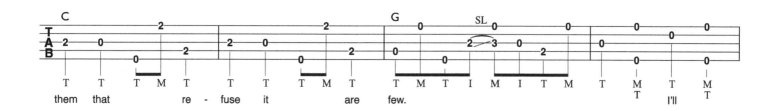

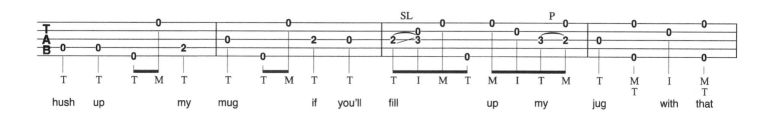

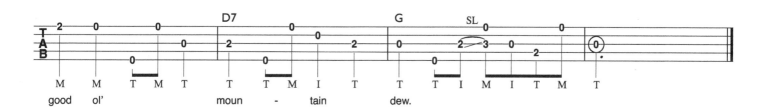

If you're familiar with "Banks of the Ohio," then you know it's one of those classic happy-sounding bluegrass murder ballads that's also a bluegrass *standard*. Certain songs are called "standards," because they are well known to audiences and are played and recorded by many artists. There are standards in many genres of music, including jazz, blues, classical, pop, folk, etc. In bluegrass music, standards are most likely to be played in jam sessions, because almost everyone knows them.

This version of "Banks of the Ohio" uses the slide lick with a forward-reverse roll and the forward roll, alternating with measures of quarter notes playing the melody. Make sure to keep the same number of beats in the measures with quarter note. In other words, don't speed up. Keep the tempo even.

BANKS OF THE OHIO

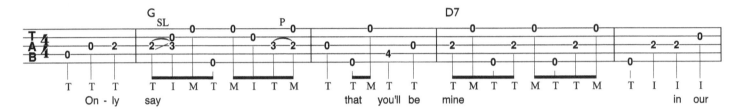

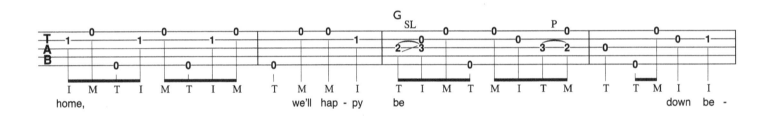

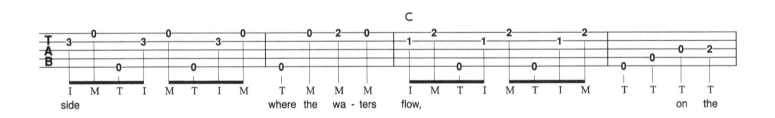

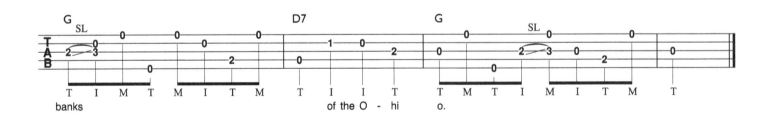

4TH-STRING SLIDE

Here's a really useful lick that involves a long slide on the 4th string. Start the slide with T and then play the 3rd string with I just as you reach the end of the slide on the 5th fret.

When used at the beginning of a song, this lick is often preceded by a couple of pickup notes. It's a great lick to use when the melody starts on the open 3rd-string G note.

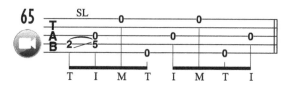

This well-known tune uses the 4th-string slide to lead into the melody, along with a couple of fill-in licks and plenty of slides.

WILL THE CIRCLE BE UNBROKEN?

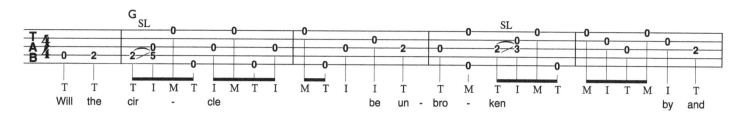

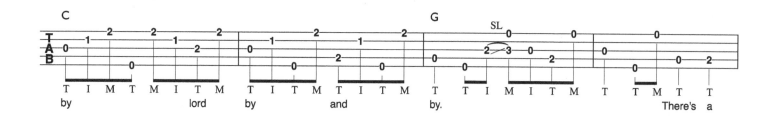

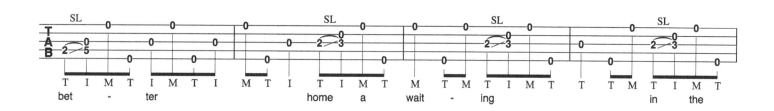

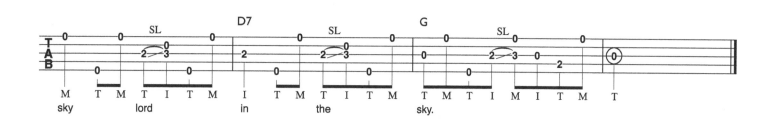

Here's another oldie but goodie. If the fill-in notes (the notes between the melody notes) are a little confusing, you can omit them and just play the melody notes as quarter notes. Then, once you've practiced the song a few times, try to fit them back in.

SHE'LL BE COMING 'ROUND THE MOUNTAIN

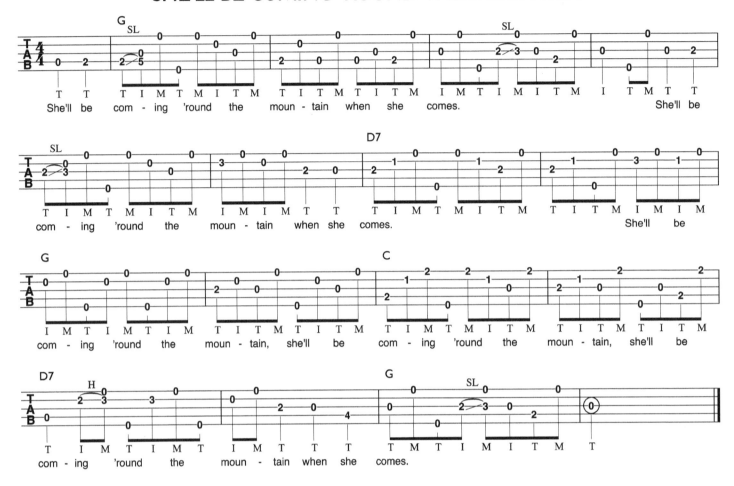

LESSON 7: INTROS AND ENDINGS

INTROS

Intros are licks that are used to lead into the melody at the beginning of a song. They also help establish the tempo. Intro licks generally walk up or down to the first melody note.

This walk-up lick would work perfectly as the intro to "Will the Circle Be Unbroken."

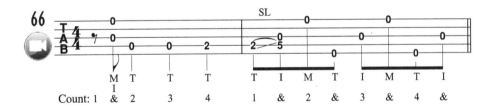

Similarly, this next one would walk up nicely to the beginning of "Grandfather's Clock," which starts on the open 3rd string but without the slide.

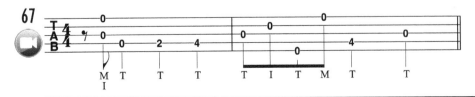

Rests
The ⁷ symbol is an *eighth rest*. A rest has the same time value as the type of note it replaces, but no note is played. You will also encounter a *quarter rest* ⌡, a *half rest* ▬, and a *whole rest* ▬.

The intro doesn't always have to directly precede the melody as long as the pickup notes take you to the note that starts the song like the next example, which would walk down to the open 4th string (D) for the first note of "Good Ol' Mountain Dew." Here's how you would count it:

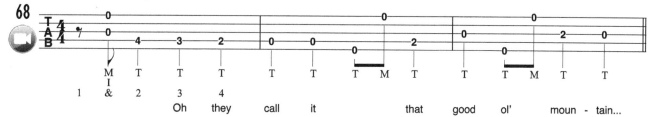

Ex. 69 begins with a quarter rest (silence for the duration of a quarter note) and walks you right in to the "Foggy Mountain" lick.

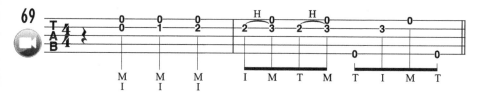

ENDINGS

Here are a couple of *endings* you could use to finish a song. This first one works perfectly at the end of "Cripple Creek." The slide from the 2nd to 5th fret is exactly the same as the opening slide of the song. The last two bars of "Cripple Creek" are included here to show you how it fits.

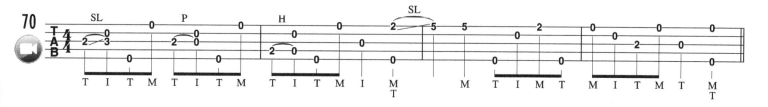

This ending is often followed by the "Shave and a Haircut" ending, which is a famous melody you're sure to recognize. Here's an easy way to play it:

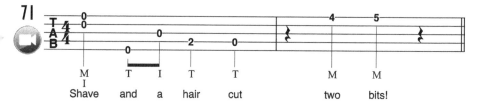

And if you're feeling brave, here's the "Shave and a Haircut" ending up high on the neck. Use your 3rd finger at the 11th fret of the 2nd string, and your 1st finger at the 9th fret of the 1st string. Your 1st finger plays the 9th and 7th frets of the 3rd string and then moves all the way up to the 16th and 17th frets for the "two bits."

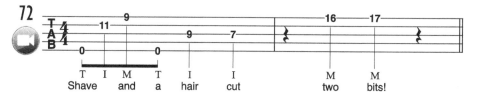

Here's an arrangement of "Lonesome Road Blues" with intro and ending licks.

LONESOME ROAD BLUES (NO. 1)

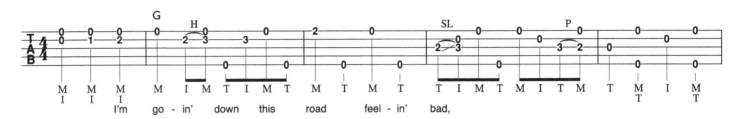

I'm go - in' down this road feel - in' bad,

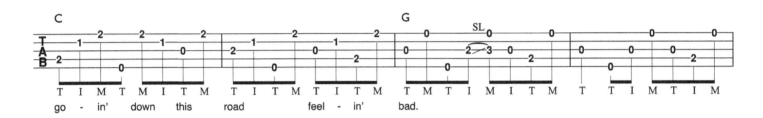

go - in' down this road feel - in' bad.

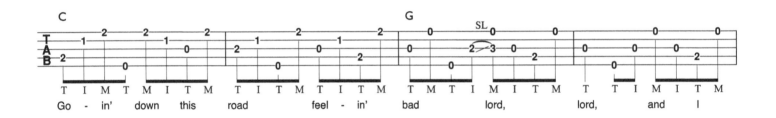

Go - in' down this road feel - in' bad lord, lord, and I

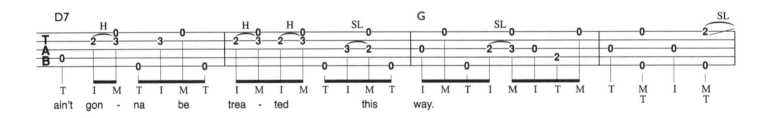

ain't gon - na be trea - ted this way.

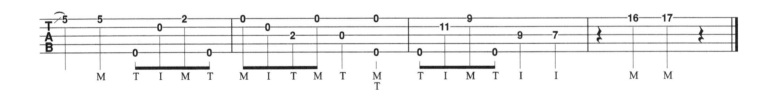

Here's another ending that will work perfectly for a vocal song. It works best when the last note of the melody is on the open 3rd string.

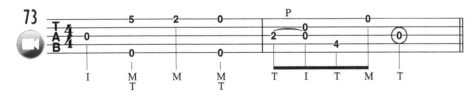

This old time number, "Long Journey Home," is also known as "Two Dollar Bill." The TAB for this song features the walk-down intro, a couple of slide/pull-off combinations, and the vocal-song ending we just learned. If you know the lyrics to this one, after you've played through the solo, strum the chords and sing along. Play two strums per measure, and try to maintain the same tempo as the solo.

 # LONG JOURNEY HOME

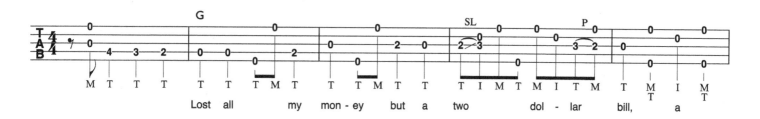

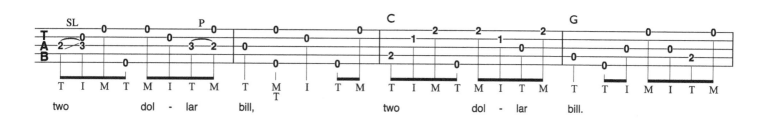

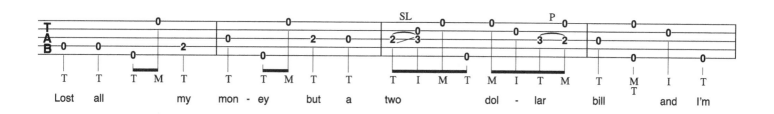

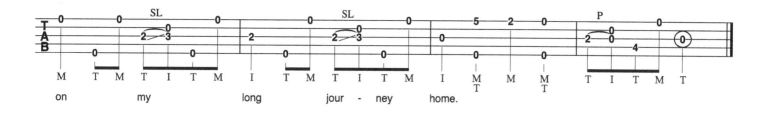

CHAPTER 5

More Chords

In Chapter 2, we learned about open chords, which are chord shapes that use both open and fretted strings. Now we're going to learn about *closed-position chords,* which do not use open strings. The good news is that, although there are many, they're all the same! Well, sort of. Let's take a look at them.

There are three basic chord shapes for making *major* chords on the banjo, and every other chord is a variation of one of these shapes. (We'll cover chords and the major scale in depth starting on page 50). The 5th string is not usually fretted (and sometimes not played) when playing chords, so there are really only four strings to hold down—one string per finger. It works out perfectly!

Here are the three basic chord shapes:

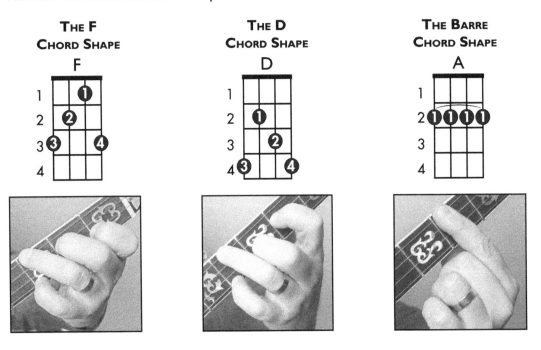

THE F CHORD SHAPE	THE D CHORD SHAPE	THE BARRE CHORD SHAPE
F	D	A

Why Are They Called That?

The *F chord shape* is called that because F is the lowest position on the banjo fretboard where that shape can be played. The *D chord shape* is similarly named, although one position lower you can play the same shape as a C♯ chord, but D is a more common chord in the banjo world, so most people call the shape after the D chord. *Barre* chords (also called bar chords) mean exactly what it sounds like: you hold your finger across all of the strings like a bar. The "barre" spelling is traditional and comes from old English or possibly French. Today, either spelling is accepted, and when pronounced out loud, they sound the same.

The beauty of closed-position chords is that without any open strings ringing, you can move the position to another place on the neck, and you'll have a different chord. As long as you know the musical alphabet (Chapter 1, Lesson 8), you can call the chord by the next note every time you move the chord up one step (a half step or whole step, depending on where you are in the alphabet).

MOVING THE BARRE CHORD SHAPE

Start with the open strings, and remember the banjo is tuned to a G chord. If you play the barre chord shape at the 1st fret, you have moved the chord up one half step to G♯/A♭. Move it up one more half step to the 2nd fret, and you've gone a whole step and are now making an A chord.

MOVING THE F AND D CHORD SHAPES

The same holds true for the other two chord shapes. If you start with the F chord as shown and move the whole chord one fret higher (a half step) you will be playing an F♯/G♭ chord. Move up one more fret and you're at G.

Now let's try a similar exercise with the D chord. Make the D chord shape as shown on the previous page and move it down (toward the nut) one fret. Now you are playing a C♯ chord. Move that one down one fret and you'll notice that your 1st finger is no longer on the fretboard (it would be playing the string at the "0" fret, or the nut). You can see now that you are playing the open-position C chord that we learned in Chapter 2, but with different fingers. So you can see that the open-position C chord is the D chord shape with an open string.

SWITCHING CHORDS

The next couple of lessons will deal with how chords are constructed and named. We'll get back to more playing techniques in a bit, but in the meantime let's discuss something important for you to start practicing now: how to switch between chords easily.

Switching between the G chord (F chord shape) and D chord (D chord shape) is a very common move in banjo playing and one that must be mastered. The difficulty for most people is keeping the 3rd finger down on the 4th string. Here's a tip for how to practice this: Make the G chord in the F chord shape at the 5th fret as shown below and, without lifting your 3rd or 4th fingers, switch your 1st and 2nd finger to the D chord shape. You'll now be making an E♭ chord, which may sound a little funny after the G, but don't worry about that for now. Once you've mastered this, switching from G to D will be much easier.

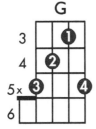
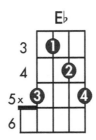

To understand how chords are made, you must first understand the *major scale*. A scale is an arrangement of notes in a specific order of whole and half steps. The major scale was made famous by the song "Do-Re-Mi" from the musical, *The Sound of Music*. There is a specific order of half steps and whole steps from which the major scale is made, and once you know the formula, you can play any major scale as long as you know the first note. The piano keyboard is a great way to visualize the major scale.

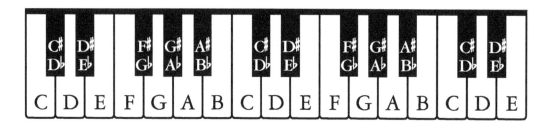

Looking at the piano keyboard diagram above, start at the C note and as you go up the keyboard (toward the right), hitting only the white keys (the natural notes), you will see the step formula for a major scale, which is as follows:

Whole–Whole–Half–Whole–Whole–Whole–Half

The C Major scale is simple as it doesn't include any sharp or flat notes. Let's try the same formula for a G Major scale. Start on the G note and follow the formula of half and whole steps. When you get to the E note, you still need to go a whole step, which takes you to F♯, then another half step to get to the next G. Notice that the last note of a major scale is always the same note name as the first. If you start a major scale on G, you'll end on G. If you start on D, you'll end on D. Now let's try this on the banjo fretboard.

THE G MAJOR SCALE

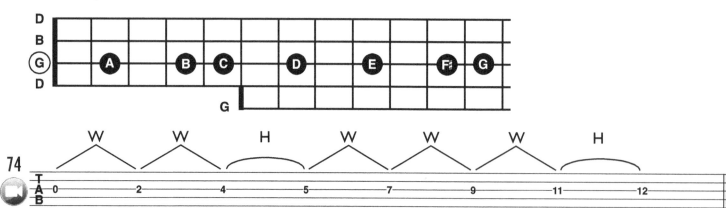

74

As you follow the pattern of whole steps and half steps above, you will get the G Major scale. It is called that because G is the *tonal center* of the scale. The tonal center is the note, or tone, the scale comes to a rest on—which is more commonly known as the *key*. For example, if a song uses notes from the G Major scale, and tends to come to rest on the G note, it is in the *key of G*. The note for which the scale is named is also called the *tonic*, although most folk, rock, and bluegrass musicians call it the *root*.

DERIVING THE MAJOR TRIAD FROM THE MAJOR SCALE

If we number the notes of the G Major scale, it looks like this:

1	2	3	4	5	6	7	8
G	A	B	C	D	E	F♯	G

The most basic kind of chord has just three notes and is called a *triad*. A *major triad* is made up of three notes from the major scale: the 1st (or root), 3rd, and 5th notes of the scale (we would simply say "1, 3, and 5"). So a G Major chord contains the notes G, B, and D. We can think of these as being the root, 3rd, and 5th of the G chord. When you strum all five open strings of the banjo, you get a G Major chord (G–D–G–B–D) with the root (G) and 5th (D) doubled.

Try the same thing for a C Major scale and see what notes make up a C Major chord.

1	2	3	4	5	6	7	8
C	D	E	F	G	A	B	C

C

E G C E

LESSON 3: CHORD INVERSIONS

A chord *inversion* is a chord with something other than the root in the bass. As you learned in the Alternating Roll lesson on page 27, the bass is the lowest-pitched note. The bass note is very important in chords.

In the G Major chord we created above, the notes were G, B, and D. If we were to change the order of the notes and play B (the 3rd) as the bass note, the order would be B, D, and G. This is called *first inversion*. Likewise, if we played the chord as D, G, and B, with the 5th in the bass, it would be *second inversion*.

The G chord in the F shape at the 5th fret is the root-position G chord. (Note: It is common to refer to major chords simply by their letter name. So, "G chord" is the same as "G Major chord.") The note played on the 4th string (the bass note) is G. The note played on the 3rd string, 4th fret is B, and the note on the 2nd string, 3rd fret is D. The 1st string at the 5th fret is also a G, the same note as the root but an *octave* higher, which means it's the same note at the other end of the scale but in a higher range.

Now make the D chord shape as shown to the right. This is the first-inversion G chord. You can check it by starting at the D chord and moving up one fret at a time, reciting the musical alphabet as you go until you get to G.

Next make the barre chord shape at the 12th fret. This is the second-inversion G chord. It is twelve half steps away from the open strings, so each note is one octave away from the open notes.

Here's a handy formula for finding all the inversions of the G chord:

- Start with the barre chord shape (open strings).
- Move up five frets and make the F chord shape with your 3rd and 4th fingers at the 5th fret (that's G again).
- Now move that chord up four frets so that your 3rd and 4th fingers are at the 9th fret. Invert your 1st and 2nd fingers to make the D shape, and you're playing a G chord again.
- Now move up three frets and make the barre shape at the 12th fret, and you're back to G once more.

Now continue the pattern:

Move up five frets from the 12th fret so that your 3rd and 4th fingers are at the 17th fret and make the F chord shape. It's the octave of the 5th fret G. Then move up four frets—you'll see that the pattern keeps going until you run out of frets!

Now try the same thing starting with the barre chord at the 5th fret for a C chord. Move up five frets, then four, then three, and you'll soon be playing all of the C chords on the banjo. (Note: To find the inversions on lower frets, use the same formula in reverse.)

Root Position G

G B D G

First Inversion G

B D G B

Second Inversion G

D G B D

LESSON 4: CHORD PROGRESSIONS

A *chord progression* is the movement of one chord to the next, or put another way, it's the order in which the chords change to follow the melody of a song. Since the banjo is tuned to a G chord, all of the songs we've learned in this book so far have been in the key of G, where the tonal center of the songs are based on notes of the G Major scale. The chords we've used have been G, C, and D (actually D7, and we'll explain what that means very soon, but for now, let's just call it D). These chords have a special relationship with each other and are known as the 1, 4, and 5 chords.

THE 1, 4, AND 5 CHORDS

Using the same system of numbering the notes of the scale, you'll see in the G Major scale that the notes G, C, and D are note numbers 1, 4, and 5 (also called the 1st, 4th, and 5th *scale degrees*). Many songs in Western music (bluegrass, country, folk, rock, jazz, blues, etc.) use chord progressions based on the 1, 4, and 5 chords. In classical music theory and in other music theory texts, you'll also see chords referred to as Roman numerals (1, 4, and 5 become I, IV, and V). It means basically the same thing, but for our purposes, we'll stick to 1, 4, and 5.

Being able to change between the 1, 4, and 5 chords (in closed-position chords) is essential for accompanying a song (either accompanying yourself singing or backing up another person). And being able to refer to the chords as 1, 4, and 5 will come in handy when playing songs in other keys (which we'll also get to soon). For now, we'll concentrate on "making the changes" in the key of G, which is just a fancy way to say playing through the chord changes.

LESSON 5: CHORD VAMPING

In standard music terminology, a *vamp* is a short, repeating musical phrase or chord progression that occurs while you wait for a song to begin or during some sort of pause. In banjo terminology, *vamping* is a method of playing chords in *backup* (an accompaniment) as an alternative to strumming. Vamping is played by holding a closed-position chord, playing the bass note with the right-hand thumb on beat 1 and then playing strings 1, 2, and 3 together (with T, I, and M) while loosening the grip with the left hand in order to mute, or cut the notes short, on beat 2.

In the following example, hold the closed-position G chord in the F chord shape at the 5th fret. Play the 4th string with T, and then play the other three strings with T, I, and M at the same time. Then, just after the chord is sounded, release the grip of your left hand just enough to make the sound of the chord stop ringing. Don't let go of the chord shape (keep your fingers on the strings), but leave them loose enough to produce a slightly pitched "click." The boxed notes are the muted notes.

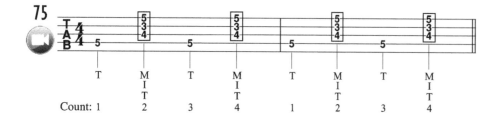

If you are familiar with playing rhythm on the guitar, then banjo vamping is similiar to the bass-chord rhythm, or "boom-chick" rhythm, of guitar strumming where the bass note is the "boom" and the muted notes are the "chick" or strum.

Vamping can be done on any of the three closed chord shapes, but since the F chord shape uses the root note as its bass note (it's in root position), we'll stick with it for a while.

Let's try vamping a simple G, C, and D chord progression using the F chord shape for all three chords: the G chord at the 5th fret, the C chord at the 10th fret, and the D chord at the 12th fret.

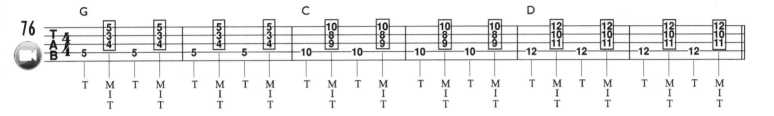

When changing chords, try to hold the chord shape with your hand and keep your fingers in contact with the strings after releasing the notes. This way, you won't make the chord change one finger at a time for each new chord. Then release all of your fingers and move them to the next chord shape simultaneously. Eventually (with repeated daily practice), you will be able to easily make chord changes while moving all of your fingers at once.

Now let's try the vamping technique on a song you already know. Instead of showing the chords in TAB, we'll use a chord chart (see page 18).

BOIL THEM CABBAGE DOWN (NO. 3)

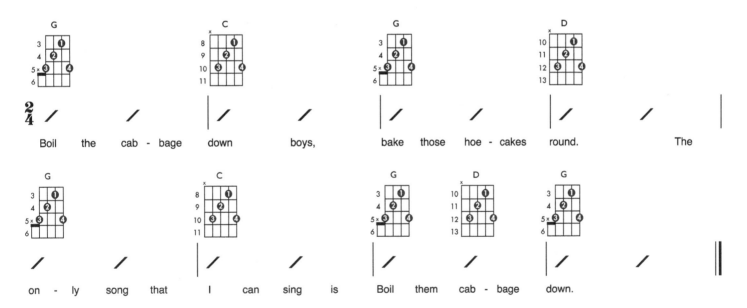

Try the same vamping pattern on any of the other songs you've learned so far. Treat the vamps as quarter notes, and play two bass-chord combinations per measure. And watch for songs where the chords change mid-measure, like in bar 7 of "Boil Them Cabbage Down." Use a few minutes of your practice time every day to practice playing and changing chords. With daily practice, your fingers will remember how to hold the chord shapes, and before long, you'll be able to change chords with your eyes closed!

A *minor chord* is constructed like a major chord in that the basic chord is a triad made of the 1st, 3rd, and 5th notes of the scale, except that in a minor chord, the 3rd is played one half step lower, or *flatted*. We often refer to this as a ♭3 ("flat-3"). Most people think of major chords as sounding happy or bright, and minor chords as sounding sad or dark. Let's go back to our major scale:

In the key of G, the major scale is built as follows:

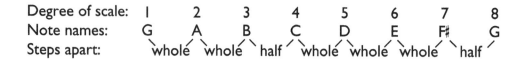

Degree of scale:	I	2	3	4	5	6	7	8
Note names:	G	A	B	C	D	E	F♯	G
Steps apart:	whole	whole	half	whole	whole	whole	half	

The third note of the G Major scale is B. To play that note flat means to play the note between A and B, which in this case is B♭. Since the G Major triad consists of the notes G, B, and D, the G Minor triad is made of G, B♭, and D. So, if you can identify the 1, 3, and 5 in each chord shape and then lower the 3rd note by one half step (one fret) to create 1, ♭3, 5, then you can turn all of the major chords into minor chords!

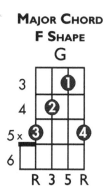

MAJOR CHORD F SHAPE
G

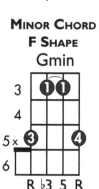

MINOR CHORD F SHAPE
Gmin

In chord charts and chord diagrams, minor chords are signified by the addition of "min" after the chord name. For example, Gmin = G Minor, Cmin = C Minor. And as we've seen so far, if only the letter name of the chord is shown (G, C, or D), you play a major chord.

The next two chord shapes include an optional fingering that uses only three strings. When vamping, sometimes (depending on the position on the neck) it's faster and easier to make just a three-string minor chord instead of the full chord shape, and it will still sound great.

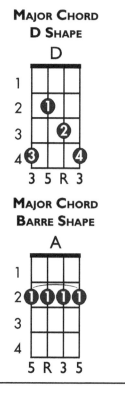

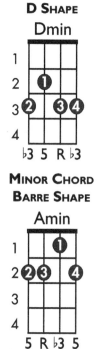

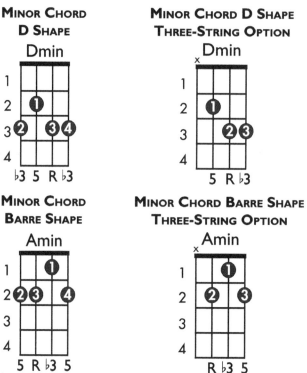

"Shady Grove" is a traditional song that is sometimes played major, and sometimes played minor. Here's an arrangement in the key of A Minor. The chords are Amin, G, and C. Learn to play the arrangement, and then work on vamping the chord changes to practice changing between the major and minor chords. Use the three-string chord for the solo and the full chord for vamping.

SHADY GROVE (ARRANGEMENT)

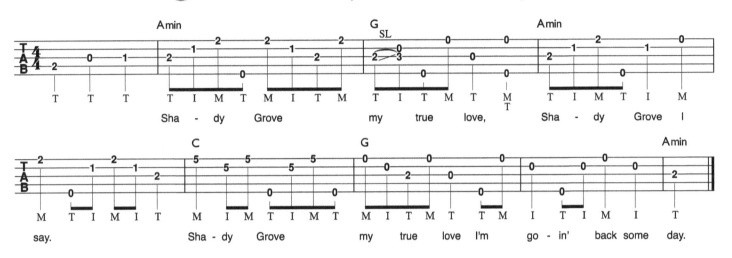

SHADY GROVE (CHORD CHANGES)

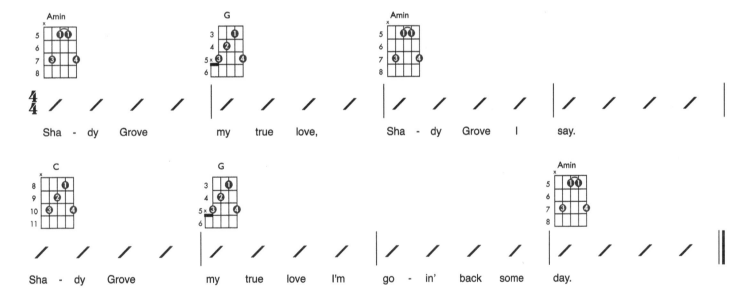

The next most common type of chord you are likely to encounter is a *7th chord*. 7th chords add a bit of extra tension, and often the 5 chord in a 1–4–5 chord progression is played as a 7th chord (like the D7 chord we learned earlier). A 7th chord is created by adding a note to the three notes of a triad, and it can be major or minor (and there are a few other variations as well). For our purposes, we will look at the most common type, which is properly known as a *dominant 7th* but most frequently just called a 7th chord. A G dominant 7th chord would be shown as "G7."

You might think that the added note would be the 7th note of the scale, and you'd be almost right! It's actually the flatted 7th note. Once again, let's go to our G Major scale:

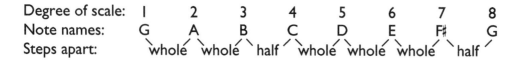

Degree of scale:	1	2	3	4	5	6	7	8
Note names:	G	A	B	C	D	E	F♯	G
Steps apart:		whole	whole	half	whole	whole	whole	half

The note we need to add to a triad to create a G7 chord is between the 6th and 7th degree of the scale, which in this case would be F-natural (F♮). There are a few other ways to finger a 7th chord on the banjo, but the examples shown below are the most common.

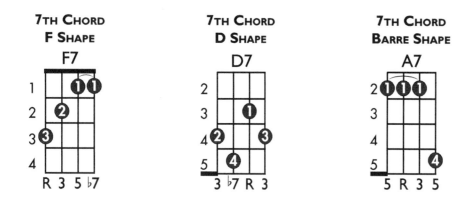

7TH CHORD F SHAPE — F7 — R 3 5 ♭7

7TH CHORD D SHAPE — D7 — 3 ♭7 R 3

7TH CHORD BARRE SHAPE — A7 — 5 R 3 5

Here's an example of a C to C7 lick with a forward-reverse roll.

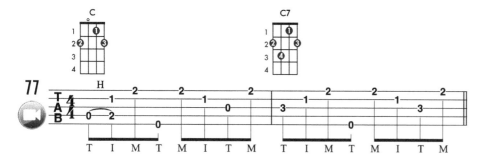

77

In the following example, the 7th is added on the 1st string while playing the open strings to make a G7 chord. As you'll see in "Lonesome Road Blues" on the next page, this lick would usually resolve into a C chord.

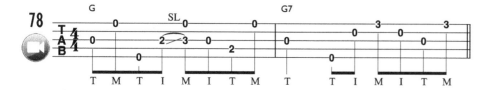

78

This version of the "Lonesome Road Blues" uses the G–G7 and C–C7 licks you just learned on page 56. Listen to how the 7th chords help you anticipate the chord changes.

LONESOME ROAD BLUES (NO. 2)

If you've ever browsed through songbooks or chord books, you've probably seen lots of other chord types, such as *diminished* (dim), *augmented* (aug), and *suspended* (sus) chords, or chords with other numbers, like *6th*, *9th*, and even *13th*. You may have wondered if you'd need a math or engineering degree to understand it all. Don't worry! While these chords all have their uses, you can get by just fine for a long time with just the chords we've learned so far. In general, the more music theory you know, the better, but a good understanding of the basics is all you really need to play. You can learn the other stuff later.

VAMPING 7TH CHORDS

Play the full versions of the 7th chords for vamping. Try vamping the chords for "Lonesome Road Blues," switching from the major chord to the dominant 7th position. Keep a steady beat throughout.

VAMPING LONESOME ROAD BLUES

I'm go - ing down this road feel - ing bad, I'm

go - in' down this road feel - ing bad. I'm

go - in' down this road feel - ing bad lord, lord, and I

ain't gon - na be trea - ted this way.

CHAPTER 6
Playing in Different Keys

LESSON 1: WHAT KEY IS THIS AND WHY CHANGE NOW?

 As we learned in Chapter 5, the key of a piece of music is determined by the chord progression and the scale used to create the melody. You could also say that the chord progression and the scale are determined by the key. Most often, the melody of a song will start on a chord, go through a few changes, and then resolve back to the original chord. This chord is usually a good indicator of the key of the song.

Since your banjo is tuned to a G chord, it's very easy to play in the key of G. All of the open strings are part of the G chord (therefore, also part of the G Major scale), and the most commonly used chords in the key of G are also easy to make and find. When playing in keys other than G, you can expect to use fewer open strings. So, why change?

One of the most common reasons to *transpose* (change the key of) a song is to accommodate a singer's vocal range. Have you ever tried to sing along with someone else and found that you had to sing either an octave lower or higher to match the notes that they were singing? This often happens when men and women, or children and adults, sing together. Or, have you ever tried to sing a song that seemed to start out fine, but then the melody went too high or low for you to sing? ("The Star-Spangled Banner" is a famous example of this.) You can sometimes find a range that better fits you by moving the song to a different key.

Also, just like many banjo tunes are written in G to accommodate the open strings of the banjo, many tunes were written for the fiddle or the mandolin are in the keys of A or D to accommodate the open strings of those instruments. When the time comes for you to play with other musicians and singers, you'll probably need to be able to play in some other keys. We'll learn a few ways to do this in this chapter.

LESSON 2: THE CAPO

 An easy way to change the key of a song is to use a *capo*. A capo is a device that attaches to the neck of a string instrument and holds the strings down at a determined fret, thereby raising the pitch of all the strings at once. Capos come in several different varieties and types, but they all basically do the same thing: hold the strings down like a barre chord. Since your banjo is tuned to a G chord, placing the capo at the 2nd fret raises the pitches of the strings a whole step to an A chord. Now, when you play songs in open position, they will come out in the key of A. Placing the capo at the 3rd fret will raise it to B♭, while the 4th fret gives you B, and the 5th fret is C, etc. Most banjo players don't use the capo higher than the 5th fret (although there are some exceptions).

Here are a few different types of capos:

PHOTO COURTESY OF SHUBB CAPOS

5TH-STRING CAPO

Because of the unique nature of the 5-string banjo (the 5th string), one capo just isn't enough. Once you use a capo to raise the pitch of the other four strings, you'll need to also raise the pitch of the 5th string by the same amount. The two most common types of 5th-string capos are the *sliding 5th-string capo* and *HO gauge model railroad spikes*. Both of these options require modification of your banjo, and should be installed by a qualified repairperson.

The sliding 5th-string capo works by sliding the capo along a track that is installed on the side of the banjo neck, letting the capo press the string down just behind the selected fret.

Sliding 5th-string capo.

As indicated by their name, the model railroad spikes are a scaled-down version of real railroad spikes and are usually used in model railroad sets. To use them, press the string down to the fingerboard (you may need to use your fingernail or fingerpick to do this), then slide the string under the open end of the railroad spike.

5th-string railroad spikes.

Capos and Chords

When you place the capo at the 2nd fret and play the open strings, an A chord is sounded instead of the usual G. When you finger an open-position C chord with the capo at the 2nd fret, it too is raised a whole step, so now a D chord is sounded. When playing closed-position chords, you must also raise them by the same amount. This is one reason it's good practice to call chords by their numbers instead of proper note names. For example, if you are playing with a guitarist and both of you are using a capo at the same fret, you might be tempted to call the chords G, C, and D, but if there are other musicians *not* using capos (mandolin players don't usually use a capo and there's no capo for a fiddle or bass), it's better form to call the chords by their numbers: the 1, 4, and 5 chords.

HOW TO USE A CAPO

With whichever type of capo you choose, here's how to make it work:

1. First decide which key you need to play in and where to place the capo.
2. Place the capo just behind the fret—but not on the fret—and tighten it down just enough so that the strings don't buzz and you get a clean, clear sound. If you overtighten the capo, you can pull the strings out of tune (if your capo is not adjustable, there's not much you can do about this).
3. A little retuning is normal after installing a capo, but if you're going really far out of tune, you may want to start over.

LESSON 3: PLAYING IN THE KEY OF C

In the previous lesson, we learned that by placing a capo at frets 2, 3, 4, and 5, the keys of A, B♭, B, and C, respectively, were easily accessible—but what about the other keys? Placing your capo at the 5th fret allows you to play in the key of C using the same techniques and licks that you would use for the key of G, but playing in the key of C *without* a capo is also fairly easy. And once you know how to play in the key of C, you would then be able to play in the keys of D, E♭, E, and F by using the capo at frets 2, 3, 4, and 5.

The keys of G and C are closely related keys, because they share many of the same notes. In the key of G, the 1, 4, and 5 chords are G, C, and D. In the key of C, they are C, F, and G. The two keys have two chords in common. What this means to a banjo player is that you can still make good use of the open strings in the key of C.

Remember, to transpose a piece of music means to change its key, or pitch. Let's transpose the melody of "Red River Valley" from the key of G to the key of C. We'll take a look at the theory involved, as well as a few practical ways of doing this on the banjo.

First, let's look at the melody of "Red River Valley" in the key of G. The example below begins with a half rest, which is silence for the duration of a half note. In measure 4, the second note (open 3rd string) uses a new note value called a *dotted half note*. Dotted notes are notes with a small dot after them. The dot increases the duration of the note it's attached to by half of its value. So, a dotted half note equals a half note (two beats) plus half of its value (one beat) to total three beats.

RED RIVER VALLEY IN G

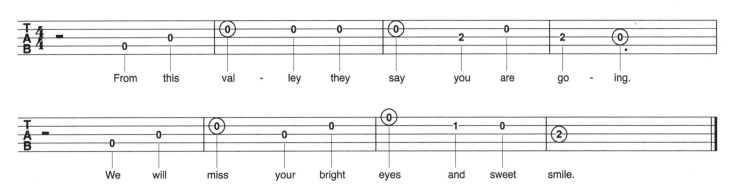

To transpose this song to the key of C, we will need to raise the pitch of each note by the same amount, as if we were using a capo at the 5th fret. One way to do this is to play every note five frets higher, like this:

RED RIVER VALLEY IN C (NO. 1)

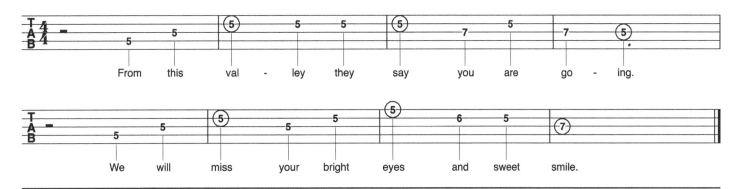

The next step is to find a way to play this melody in another location. The first three notes of this song in the key of G are played on the open 4th, 3rd, and 2nd strings (D, G, and B). As we learned on page 51, these are the three notes that make up a G Major triad (5th, root, and 3rd). Playing these strings at the 5th fret (C barre chord) changes the pitch of the notes to G, C, and E (5th, root, and 3rd of a C chord). Now try it by fretting the first-position C chord, starting the melody on the open 3rd string (which is the same note as the 4th string, 5th fret).

RED RIVER VALLEY IN C (NO. 2)

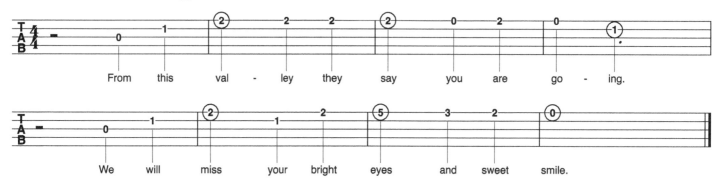

"Red River Valley in C (Arrangement)" includes rolls and fill-ins. You'll also notice that, since quite a bit of the melody has moved to the 1st string, more backward rolls are used. This keeps you from having to play the 1st string twice consecutively during a roll.

RED RIVER VALLEY IN C (ARRANGEMENT)

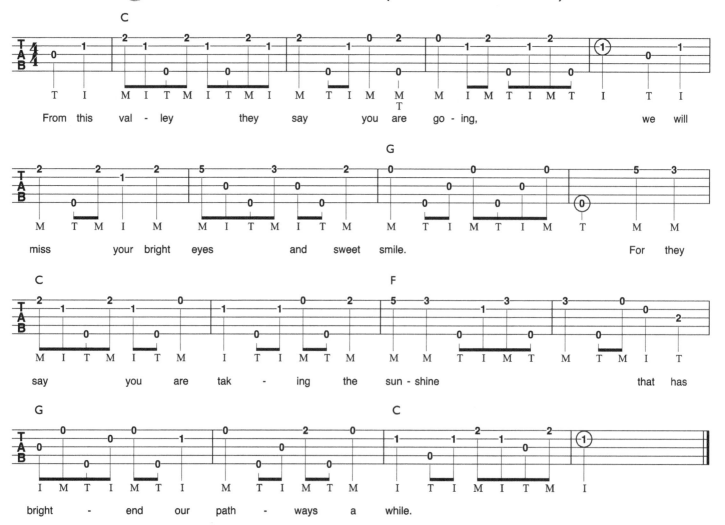

LESSON 4: DROP C TUNING

Another option for playing in keys other than G is to change the tuning of the strings. *Drop C tuning* is so named because the 4th string is dropped from D down to C. Before the days of bluegrass music, this was actually a more common tuning for the banjo than the now-standard G tuning. In the late 1800s and early 1900s (often called the "classic banjo era"), marches, polkas, rags, and even classical music were played on the banjo in drop C tuning.

To tune your banjo to drop C tuning, you must lower the pitch of the 4th string one whole step from D to C. You can either use an electronic tuner for this, or to use the fret-matching method—your 4th string, 7th fret should match the 3rd string open.

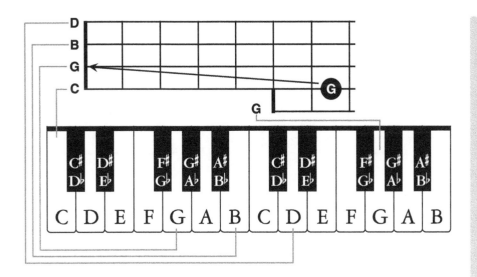

A Note About Changing Tunings on the Banjo

Once you've changed the tuning of one or more strings, you may find that the other strings (the ones you haven't changed) are now slightly out of tune. This is due to the flexibility of the banjo head. When the tension of one string is changed, it changes the amount of pressure pushing down on the bridge and head, which changes the tension on the strings and can cause them to go out of tune. So, once you've tuned one string, you should check all of them.

CHORD FINGERINGS FOR DROP C TUNING

To make a C chord in drop C tuning, leave your 4th string open. To make an F chord, leave the 4th string open, and in place of a G chord, we'll use a G7 chord as shown below.

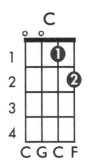
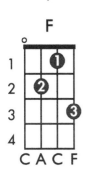
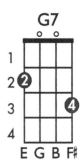

Let's try a roll exercise with these new chord shapes.

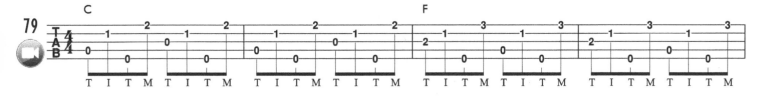

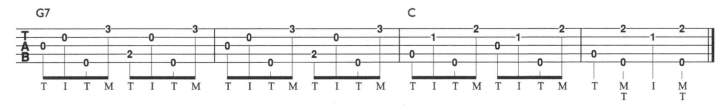

"Soldier's Joy" is a traditional fiddle tune that is also a jam session favorite for mandolin and guitar players. It is played in the key of D, and for this arrangement, we will play the song using drop C tuning. Place your capo at the 2nd fret to play this song in the key of D (and remember you must also use a capo on your 5th string).

Part B of "Soldier's Joy" contains a couple of barre positions (in measures 1 and 2 of Part B). Finger them as shown with your 3rd finger on the 1st string, and 2nd finger on the 2nd string. This way, your 2nd finger stays on the 1st string after playing the C chord. It may take a little time to get used to this new position, but it will make for a faster change than fretting those notes with your 1st finger.

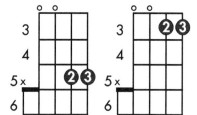

SOLDIER'S JOY

Drop C tuning
Capo 2nd fret to play in the key of D

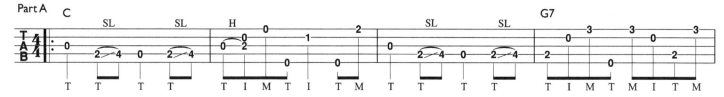

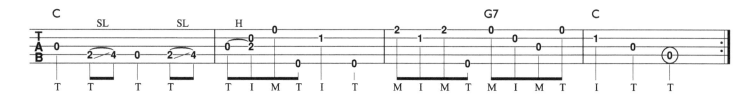

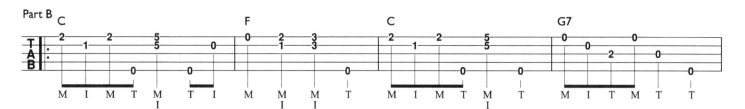

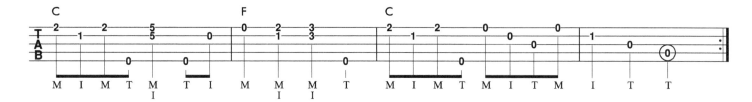

Note the repeat signs. Like many fiddle tunes, the A and B parts of "Soldier's Joy" are both repeated. Instead of using two pages to print this tune, the repeat signs made it possible to print it on one. Very economical!

Like the key of C, the key of D is closely related to the key of G, so the key of D also lends itself to being played in standard G tuning without too much trouble. With a capo at the 2nd, 3rd, and 4th frets in G tuning, playing in the D position will allow you to play in the keys of E, F, and F♯. Combined with the open G position and the key of C position, this gives the banjo player access to all 12 keys while still maintaining the open string sound of the banjo. The 1, 4, and 5 chords for the key of D are D, G, and A.

Another trick that banjo players like to use for playing in the key of D is to capo just the 5th string at the 7th fret to raise the pitch to A. This enables us to use the 5th string as an open string because the D chord (the tonic chord for the key of D) contains an A note (a D Major triad is D–F♯–A). The capoed open 5th string sounding the note A works for the 1 chord (D) and the 5 chord (A), but an open 5th string without a capo sounding the note G would not work as well since G is only found in the 4 chord (G).

Here's an old-time tune that's a jam session standard in the key of D featuring lots of open strings. This arrangement of "Angeline the Baker" is in standard G tuning with the 5th string capoed at the 7th fret. If you don't have a 5th-string capo, you can tune the 5th string up a whole step to A.

ANGELINE THE BAKER

Capo 5th string at 7th fret

Using "Red River Valley," let's take a look at how a familiar melody works in the key of D. This one is going to be a little tougher since much of the melody is on the first two strings, and there won't be as many open strings to use. It will be good practice for holding the D chord though.

For measures 2 and 3 of the second line, use the same fingering that you used for the barre positions in "Soldier's Joy," with your 3rd finger on the 1st string and 2nd finger on the 2nd string. This is a faster position to get to and since you're not playing the other notes of the barre chord, there's no need to hold them down. Once again, putting a capo on your 5th string, 7th fret to raise the pitch to A will sound best for this key.

RED RIVER VALLEY (KEY OF D)

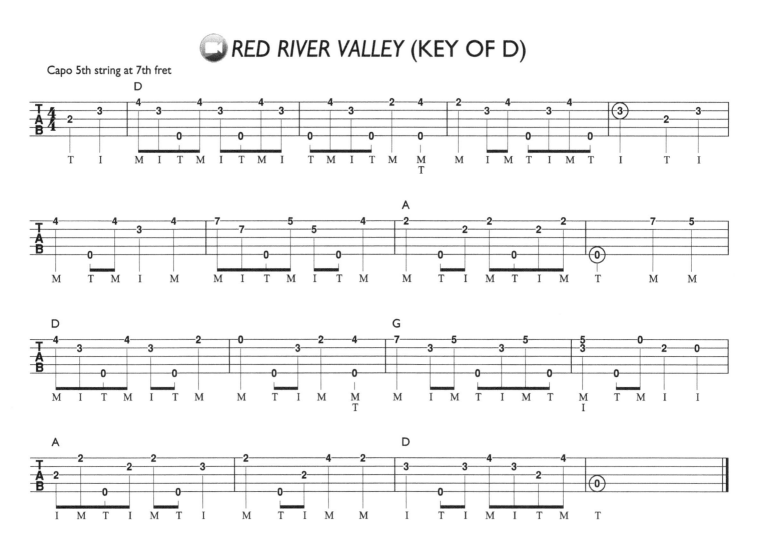

Now that you've played a couple of tunes in the keys of C and D, go back to some of the songs that we've done in G and see if you can find the melody in C or D. Start by holding the chord and singing the melody, then look for the notes that you sang. For extra credit, try to work them into an arrangement with rolls and fill-in licks!

In *D tuning*, you will be tuning your banjo to a D chord so when you strum the open strings, it will sound full D chord. The strings will be tuned to the notes (from 1st to 5th) D–A–F♯–D–F♯. Start with your 4th string tuned to D (like in G tuning), and then follow the diagram for the fret-to-fret tuning:

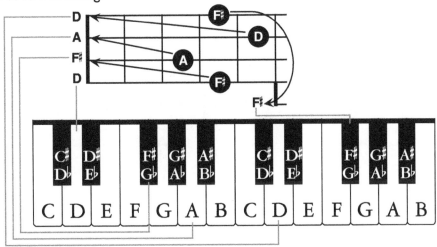

D tuning is not used as often as G tuning and possibly not even as much as drop C tuning, but there are a number of specialty tunes worth knowing that are usually played in D tuning. Since you'll be playing in the key of D, you'll want to know open-position chords for the 1, 4, and 5 chords in D, which are D, G, and A. D is played on the open strings and here are the shapes for G and A7 in D tuning:

CHORD FINGERINGS FOR D TUNING

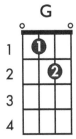

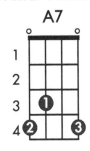

It's possible to play closed-position chords in D tuning, but since there are so few songs are played in this tuning, many banjo players use a shortcut: When vamping chords in any open tuning (where the open strings play a full chord), the barre position at the 12th fret will sound the 1 chord, the 5th fret will sound the 4 chord, and the 7th fret will sound the 5 chord. This works for G tuning, too—but don't be lazy, learn the proper chords for G!

"Rueben" is probably the most popular song in D tuning. According to bluegrass legend Earl Scruggs, this is the song he was playing when he discovered the three-finger style of picking. It's not a hard song to play, and it uses some familiar-looking licks—although they sound different in this tuning.

REUBEN

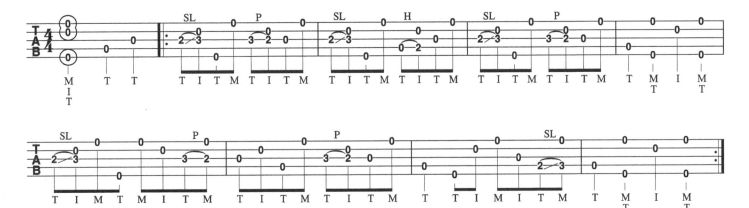

"Home Sweet Home" is a pretty easy song to play in D tuning. This time, capo your 5th string to A (7th fret). Also watch the repeat signs and the *first and second endings*. When you get to the first-ending repeat sign, go back to the repeat sign at the beginning. The second time through, skip the first ending and play the second ending, which takes you through the second part. Then follow the repeat sign for the second part and play through to the ending. It's another musical shortcut.

HOME SWEET HOME

Capo 5th string at 7th fret

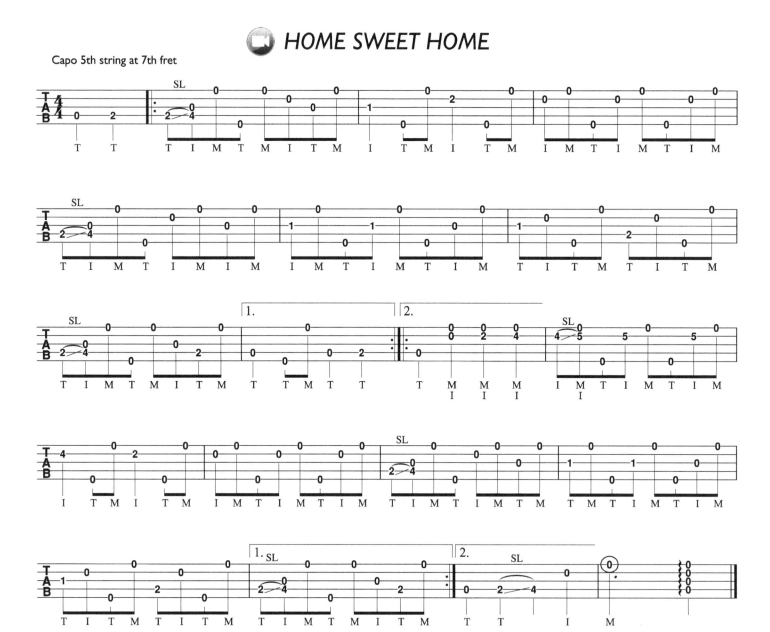

How Many Tunings Are There?

That's a good question. A banjo player once bragged that he used 13 different tunings in one show! (Although we have no idea what they all were.) For bluegrass style playing, G is by far the most common tuning. Drop C and D tunings are probably the next-most common. In old-time banjo playing (clawhammer, frailing, and *drop-thumb* styles, which we will discuss later in this book), *double C tuning* is very popular. There are also tunings for minor keys, such as *G Minor tuning* and *D Minor tuning*, and there are fun tunes that can be played in those tunings. You'll spend most of your picking time, however, in good-old G tuning, so that's where you should spend most of your practice time, too.

CHAPTER 7

Melodic Style

Melodic style is the name given to a style of banjo playing that was developed by players like Bill Keith and Bobby Thompson in the 1960s. It enabled banjo players to play scale passages and tunes based on scales more fluidly and cleanly than in either the Earl Scruggs style or in the roll style we've been playing.

We're back to playing in G tuning for this chapter. Earlier in the book, we laid out a G Major scale along one string as a demonstration of how the scale was constructed. It looked like this:

This did a pretty good job of explaining the steps involved in building a major scale, but it's a pretty inefficient way to play the scale. Here's another way to play the same notes, this time using more than one string.

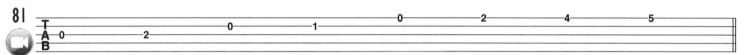

In melodic style, we play the first note of the scale on one string and then the next note on another, so that we don't play the same string twice in a row. Here's the same scale in melodic style.

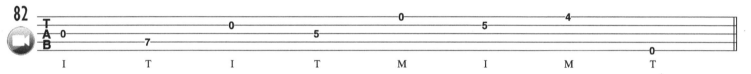

The old-time fiddle tune "Devil's Dream" offers a good example of how melodic style can be adapted to play fiddle tunes easily. Here's the melody to the first part of "Devil's Dream" played in the along-one-string style.

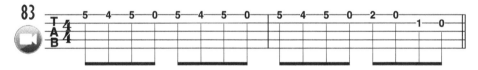

Compare that to the same notes played in melodic style.

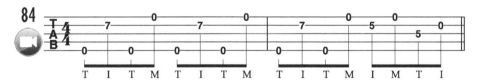

Following are a few tips on the fingering to use in "Devil's Dream."

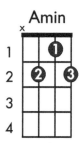

- For bars 3 and 4 of both the A and B part, you'll need to hold an Amin chord.
- For bar 3 of the second line of each part, use your 1st finger on the 5th fret of the 3rd string, and your 2nd finger on the 5th fret of the 2nd string, then after you've played the 2nd-string, 5th-fret note, use your 3rd finger to reach the 7th fret of the 4th string.

DEVIL'S DREAM

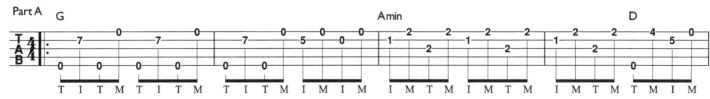

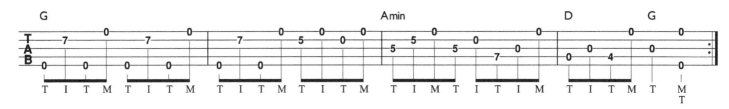

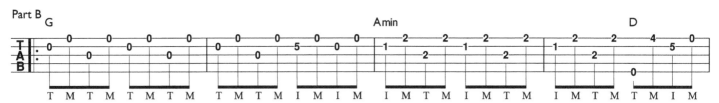

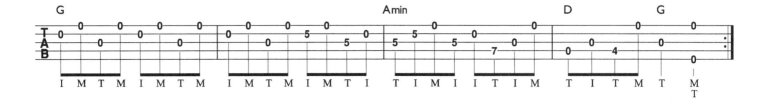

Following is a version of the tune "Cripple Creek" that we learned earlier, but this time done in melodic style. The first part starts high on the neck at the 10th and 9th frets. Use your left-hand 2nd finger to play the 2nd string, and your 1st finger to play the 1st string. Then move your fingers to the 5th and 4th frets while in the same position. Here's an easy way to remember this. There is an inlay (or dot) at the 10th fret and at the 5th fret, and those are the frets where your 2nd finger goes for this position.

CRIPPLE CREEK (MELODIC STYLE)

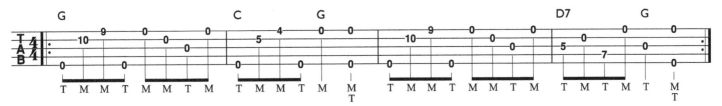

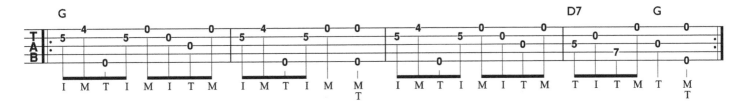

You might recognize the following tune as the melody for the Johnny Horton song "The Battle of New Orleans." The date (January 8th) is also famous for being Elvis Presley's birthday. To play the tune, you'll need to fret the 5th string with your 3rd finger at the 12th fret. The 1st and 2nd fingers stay in the same position for the first three measures. Just slide them from frets 10 and 9 to 8 and 7, then to 5 and 4.

THE EIGHTH OF JANUARY

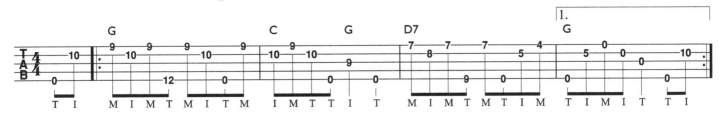

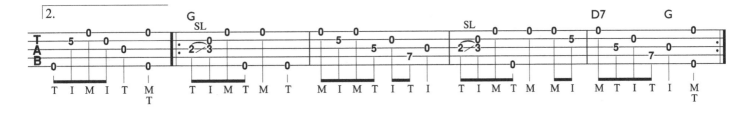

"Red-Haired Boy" is an Irish tune also known as "The Little Beggar Man." It's a very popular jam session tune, especially among guitarists, as well as fiddlers and mandolin players. Like many fiddle tunes, this one is in the key of A. You'll need to put your capo on the 2nd fret before playing this one with a fiddler, but let's first practice it in G. The chords are given in the key of G, which is common practice for songs usually done with a capo.

RED-HAIRED BOY

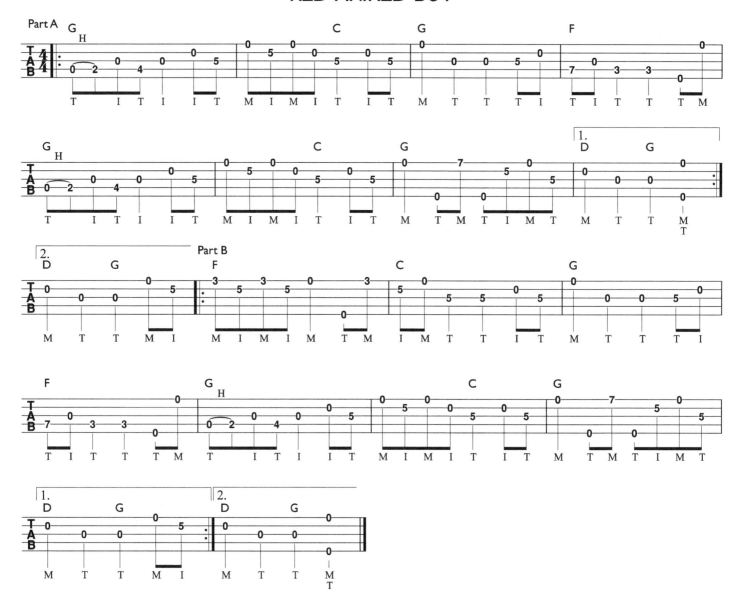

CHAPTER 8

Playing in $\frac{3}{4}$ Time

LESSON 1: INTRODUCING $\frac{3}{4}$, OR WALTZ TIME

$\frac{3}{4}$ time, or *waltz time,* as the time signature suggests, means there are only three beats per measure. Some famous waltzes you may be familiar with are "The Blue Danube Waltz" and "The Tennessee Waltz." Those are a few examples of slow waltzes, which are what first come to mind for most people with waltzes, but there are fast waltzes as well. In bluegrass music, the Stanley Brothers recorded several fast waltzes, such as "Stone Walls and Steel Bars."

With only three beats per measure, our usual banjo roll with eight eighth notes isn't going to fit evenly, so we'll have to modify some of the licks and rolls. But, at the same time, the three-finger picking style used for banjo-playing makes waltz time seem like a natural fit.

LESSON 2: $\frac{3}{4}$ ROLLS

Remember, the time signature $\frac{3}{4}$ tells you there are three beats to the measure and that a quarter note equals one beat, so an eighth-note banjo roll will turn into six notes instead of eight.

The rolls still keep their names depending on which direction the fingers are going, so T–I–M is still a forward roll.

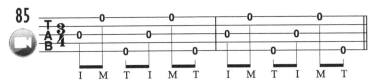

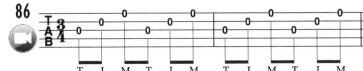

And, of course, M–I–T would be a backward roll.

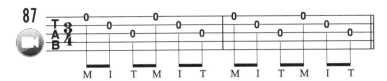

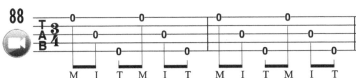

The alternating roll and forward-reverse roll each take an interesting twist in waltz time.

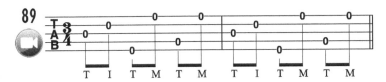

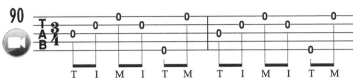

Despite the sadness implied in the title, "All the Good Times Are Past and Gone" is actually a fun song to play and a great introduction to ¾ time. Some of the licks will be familiar, but they'll feel like they go by a little faster because of the time signature change. Just keep thinking 1–2–3, 1–2–3, and you'll be fine.

ALL THE GOOD TIMES ARE PAST AND GONE

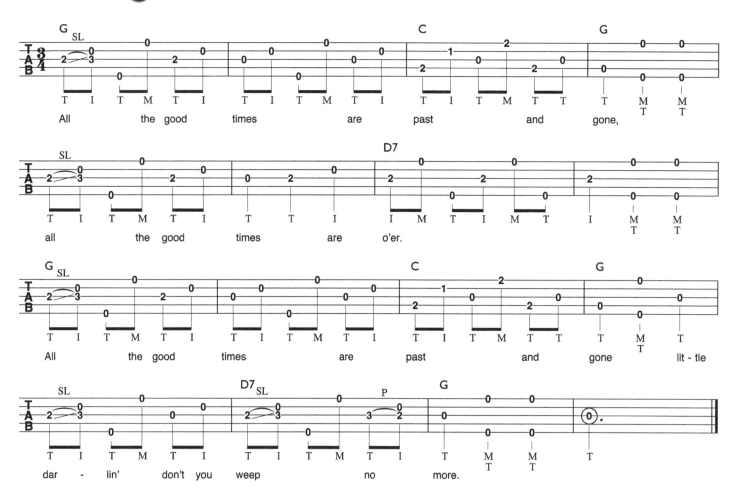

VAMPING IN ¾ TIME

When vamping chords for a ¾ time song, the thumb still plays the *downbeat* (first beat of the measure, usually the strongest beat) but is then followed by two weaker beats. Here's an excerpt from "All the Good Times Are Past and Gone" done this way:

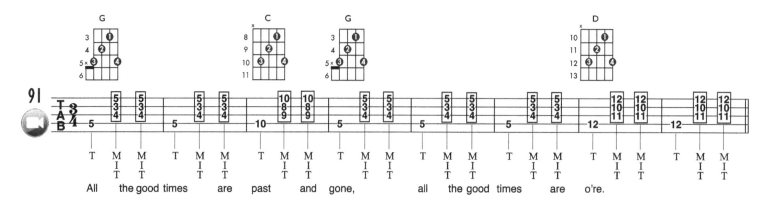

Here's another classic tune that everyone should know.

AMAZING GRACE

ANOTHER ACCOMPANIMENT OPTION

Instead of vamping the chords, try this *double-time forward roll* under the lyrics to this song.
Hold the same F chord shape and move it from G to C to D, and play the roll as shown.

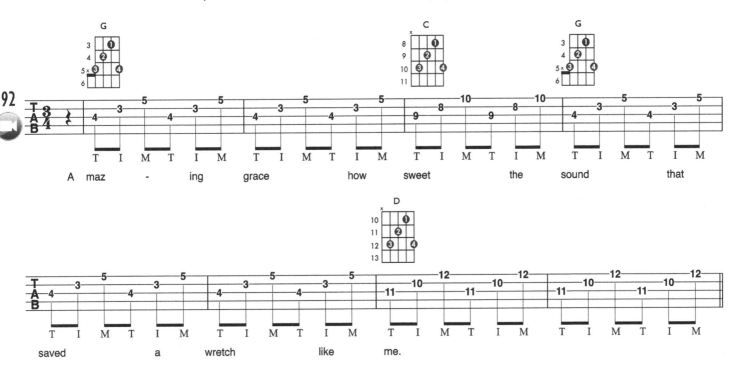

Here's one more tune in ¾ time. To play the D chord in bar 3, use your 3rd finger on the 4th string, 4th fret and your 1st finger on the 3rd string, 2nd fret. There are also places (bar 2) where you'll hold a D7 chord position even though it's not a D7 chord in the song. The melody of the song is still in G, but the notes needed also happen to be the same notes that make up a D7 chord.

GOOD NIGHT IRENE

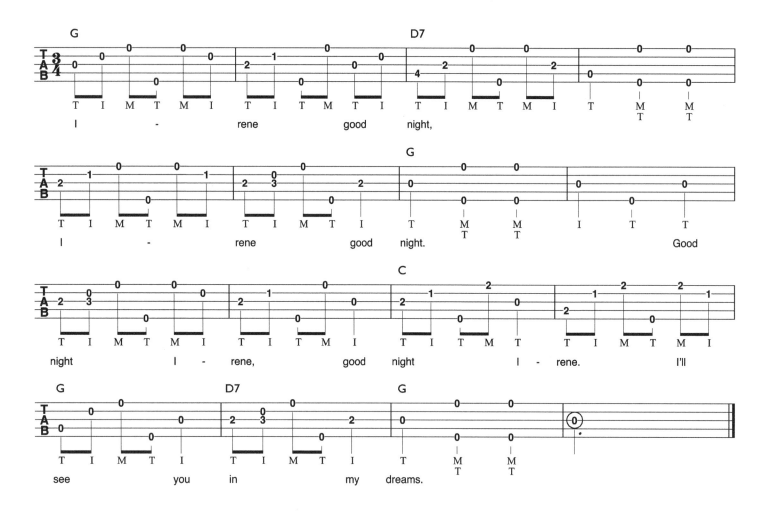

CHAPTER 9

Clawhammer and Old-Time Style

Clawhammer, frailing, and *drop-thumb* are a few of the names given to what many also call the *old-time style* of banjo playing. Banjo great Grandpa Jones called it "rapping," presumably because your knuckles will "rap" on the banjo head like knocking on a door. There are some subtle differences between the styles, but it is generally agreed that the term clawhammer covers them all.

Unlike the bluegrass-style fingerpicking that we've been playing, clawhammer is usually played without picks. Instead of picking the strings upward as we do with fingerpicks, the player uses a *downstroke* (picking downward towards the floor) with the fingernail of either the I or M finger to either brush across all the strings or to pick an individual string. The thumb mostly plays the 5th string. (In drop-thumb style, the thumb is used to play other strings as well.)

If bluegrass and fingerpicking styles are all that you're interested in, feel free to skip this chapter. Many would agree, however, that a well-rounded banjo player should be familiar with many styles of playing, and learning a new one will not interfere with any other. If you're ready to get started, then let's go!

THE RIGHT HAND

To play clawhammer style, your right hand should be relaxed but curled up. You're not quite making a fist, but imagine that you're holding a TV remote control or a chocolate bar. You'll also want to move a little farther away from the bridge than when you're fingerpicking. In fact, some clawhammer players play right over the end of the fretboard. For now, let's aim for the spot just at the end of the neck, but over the head of the banjo as shown in the photos.

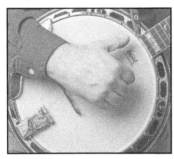 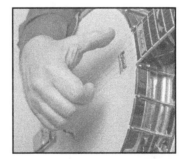

With your hand in playing position, fingers curled loosely, and wrist slightly bent, knock on the banjo head with your right-hand knuckles by moving your wrist up and down, like knocking on a door (not side to side like strumming). This is the proper motion for clawhammer playing.

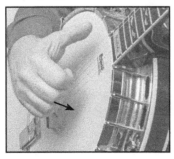 

With the clawhammer motion we just learned, take I or M (either one is correct so use whichever is most comfortable to you) and strike down with the fingernail of that finger to hit the 1st string. Your finger (or your knuckles) should come to rest on the banjo head. Do this a few times in rhythm.

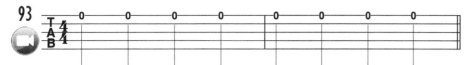

Now, using the same motion again, try striking each of the top four strings four times. Keep at it until your accuracy improves. Remember to move your hand at the wrist, and keep your fingers curled. When playing one of the inside strings (strings 2, 3, or 4), let your finger come to rest on the next string down. For example, your finger should rest on the 1st string after striking the 2nd string.

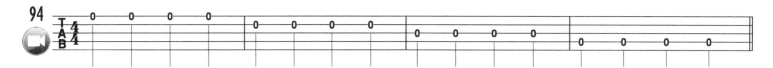

Once you are comfortable with Ex. 94, try a few different patterns. The goal is to be able to hit whichever string you want cleanly.

Open-Back vs. Resonator Banjo
You'll notice that many clawhammer banjo players prefer an open-back banjo (one without a resonator). Since the back of the banjo is directed at your body, the sound of an open-back banjo is more mellow and less bright. Some old-time players put a piece of foam rubber or a rag inside their banjo to further deaden the sound. The notes on open-back banjos tend to "pop" instead of "ring." Many old-time players prefer this sound, but some like the sound of a resonator banjo for clawhammer style. The truth is, as long as your banjo has five strings on it, you're all set! You can play either style on any 5-string banjo. Plus, you can always take the resonator off to hear how it sounds without.

The *bum-ditty* is the basic clawhammer stroke, and it gets its name from the sound it produces. If you say "bum-ditty-bum-ditty-bum-ditty-bum-ditty," you'll hear the rhythm that you're supposed to make while playing clawhammer style. There are a couple of variations, but let's learn the basics to start.

BUM

With your right hand, play a downstroke with either I or M on the 1st string, as described on the previous page, but now let your T come to rest on the 5th string once you've struck the 1st string. Your hand should still be in the claw position but is relaxed. Having your thumb on the 5th string will keep your hand from sliding off the banjo.

DITTY

To perform the "dit" in "ditty," lift your hand back up (without sounding the 5th string) and bring it down, brushing across the strings with the back of a fingernail, using either I or M. You don't have to play all of them, but at least hit the first three strings. Your thumb will again come to rest on the 5th string. To play the "ty" in "ditty," pull your hand away, playing the 5th string with T.

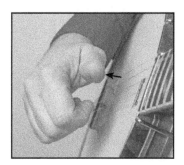

In the "ty" of "ditty," try not to make an actual picking motion with T. Your hand should be relaxed, and it should feel more like you're just lifting your hand up again; your thumb is just catching the 5th string, almost by accident. Repeat this motion slowly and keep thinking the words "bum-ditty" to keep the rhythm. It's important to keep your hand relaxed. You can also practice this rhythm with the strings muted. Keep your left hand on the strings (to mute them), and practice the right-hand rhythm while you're watching TV or something until the rhythm becomes second nature. In TAB, the "bum-ditty" rhythm looks like this:

96

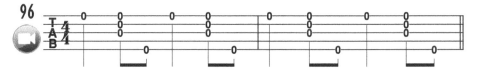

The next step is to try to hit a different string for the first stroke ("bum"). Try the 2nd string, then the 3rd, and finally the 4th string.

97

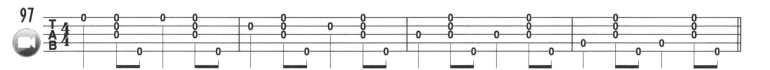

Once you're comfortable with switching strings on the first stroke, let's add some chords and play a tune. By adding the C and D7 chords, we can easily turn this into "Boil Them Cabbage Down."

BOIL THEM CABBAGE DOWN (BUM-DITTY)

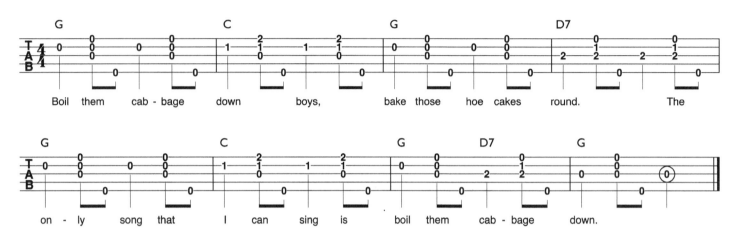

GO TELL AUNT RHODY (BUM-DITTY)

You can use the bum-ditty lick in clawhammer style like you'd use the 5th–1st fill-in that we learned back in Chapter 1. It's almost the opposite, but it's exactly the same time value. So let's try adding a melody to the chords for "Go Tell Aunt Rhody."

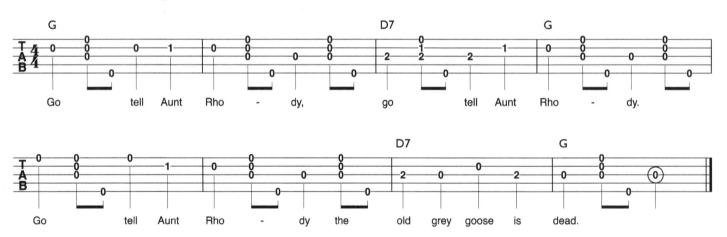

While you're practicing the bum-ditty stroke, why not apply it to music you know already? Use open-position G, C, and D7 chords with the bum-ditty stroke to play along with songs from earlier in this book. Just use two bum-dittys per measure for songs like "Good Ol' Mountain Dew," "Long Journey Home," "Red River Valley," and "Coming Around the Mountain."

Let's play a variation of the bum-ditty rhythm by replacing the strum (the "dit" of "ditty") with a downstroke on the open 1st string.

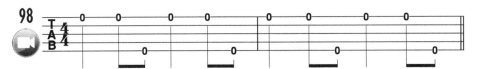

Try this one using each of the top four strings for the first stroke.

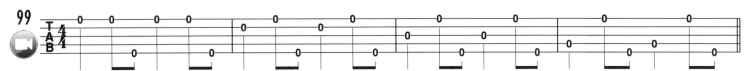

CLAWHAMMER PULL-OFFS, SLIDES, AND HAMMER-ONS

Now we're ready to start adding and combining some left-hand techniques. Play a pull-off lick by fretting the note and then pulling off the same way as you did when fingerpicking, but this time add the bum-ditty. Following are a couple of examples.

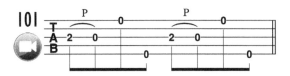

One difference between clawhammer licks and fingerpicking licks is the absence of the note picked simultaneously with the second note in the pull-off. Let's compare a clawhammer slide lick to its fingerpicking counterpart.

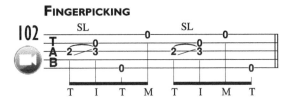

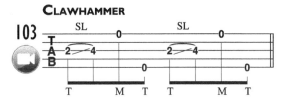

The same is true for the hammer-on lick. Remember to play the slide, pull-off, and hammer-on notes as eighth notes. This combination actually fills in the rhythm of a bum-ditty lick to make it all eighth notes, instead of quarter–eighth–eighth. Try a couple of these licks. They should seem pretty familiar by now.

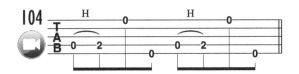

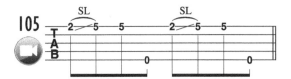

Here's a clawhammer version of "Cripple Creek." Notice that the 3rd-string slide goes all the way to the 4th fret in this version. This helps make up for the sound that's missing from the open B string that's played when we play this song bluegrass-style.

CRIPPLE CREEK (CLAWHAMMER VERSION)

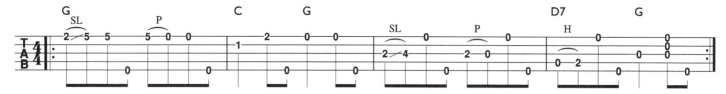

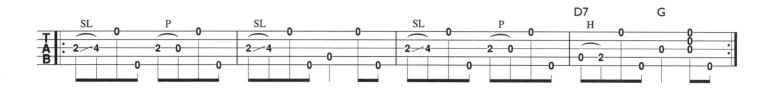

In the clawhammer version of "Cumberland Gap," you'll see a pull-off from the 4th fret of the 3rd string to the open string. This would be unusual in bluegrass-style picking, but clawhammer relies a lot on pull-offs and hammer-ons for the extra notes.

CUMBERLAND GAP (CLAWHAMMER VERSION)

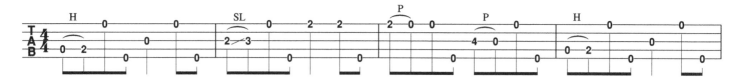

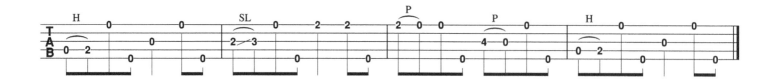

CHAPTER 10
Banjo Care and Maintenance

Banjos are one of the most adjustable and modifiable instruments in the acoustic instrument world, with many moving (and sometimes interchangeable) parts. You don't have to be a mechanic to play the banjo (it doesn't hurt), but because so many parts are adjustable or movable, it's a good idea to know a few basics to keep your banjo in proper playing shape.

LESSON 1: MORE ABOUT BANJOS

Banjos come in a few different varieties and sizes, and with different numbers of strings. Most banjos share the same body (often referred to as the pot, see page 6) but have different necks. The 5-string banjo is the one we've been learning, but let's take a look at a few others.

TENOR BANJO

The *tenor banjo* has four strings and a shorter neck than the 5-string. Tenor banjos are most often played with a flatpick (also known as a *plectrum*) and most often associated with playing Dixieland jazz and ragtime music. Tenor banjos are also popular in Irish music.

PLECTRUM BANJO

The *plectrum banjo* has four strings and the same neck length as the 5-string banjo. It's basically a 5-string without the shorter 5th string. Like the tenor, the plectrum is played with a flatpick and most often played by jazz musicians.

GUITAR BANJO

You may have seen the *guitar banjo* being played by country artists on TV. The guitar banjo has six strings and is tuned and played like a guitar. They were invented so that guitar players could get the sound of a banjo without learning to play a new instrument. Since the body is the same as a banjo, it has the same tone as a banjo. But, without the 5th string, it doesn't lend itself to the same playing style of more-traditional banjos. There are also *12-string guitar banjos*, tuned and played just like a 12-string guitar.

BANJO UKULELE

As the name implies, the *banjo ukulele* has four strings and is tuned and played like a ukulele. Most banjo ukes have a smaller head than the tenor or 5-string banjo.

MANDOLIN BANJO

The *mandolin banjo* (or *banjo mandolin*) has banjo body with a mandolin neck. Many mandolin banjos from the early 1900s and 1920s were built on the same pot as the tenor, plectrum, and 5-string.

6-STRING BANJO

Unlike the guitar banjo, which also has six strings, this one is tuned like a 5-string banjo, with a short string on top of the neck (the 6th string), but with an extra bass string between the 4th and 6th strings. There aren't many of these around.

LONG-NECK BANJO

This type of banjo is most closely associated with folk performers like Pete Seeger and the Kingston Trio. It's a 5-string banjo but with three extra frets (the 5th string attaches at around the 8th fret instead of the 5th). These banjos are tuned to an E chord instead of G, but you can place a capo at the 3rd fret to play in G.

OPEN-BACK VS. RESONATOR BANJO

One basic variation between 5-string banjos is whether they have an open back or a resonator. You can learn to play any style of banjo music on either type as long as the instrument is playable and easily tuned. Most bluegrass players prefer the louder, brighter sound of the resonator banjo, while clawhammer players often prefer the softer, mellower sound of the open-back. While there are a few banjos designed to be convertible (played both as a resonator or open-back), most are designed to be used one way or the other.

Open-back banjo.

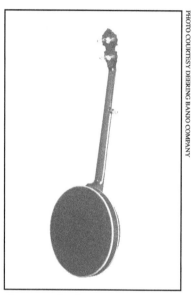

Resonator banjo.

Banjo with pop-off resonator.

PHOTO COURTESY DEERING BANJO COMPANY

TONE RINGS AND RIMS

The *rim* of your banjo is the shell that the head is stretched over. The rims in some student-model banjos are made entirely of aluminum, while some are wood. In the more intermediate-grade and professional instruments, the rim is made of wood and often capped with a *tone ring*. The tone ring is cast of metal (usually a brass or bronze alloy) and sits on top of the rim, just under the head. The tone ring usually weighs several pounds and contributes quite a bit to the weight of the banjo.

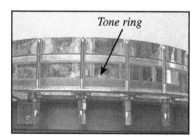

Tone ring from side.

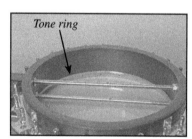

Tone ring from inside, disassembled.

Open-back banjo wood rim without tone ring.

Major repairs to any instrument should be taken to a qualified repair shop, but there are a few basic maintenance issues that you can easily take care of yourself. Check your banjo periodically to ensure that it stays in tune and is at its peak playability.

BRIDGE PLACEMENT

The bridge on your banjo is not glued in place (at least, it shouldn't be). It is held in place by the tension of the strings and can move if accidentally bumped. The placement of the bridge is critical to being in tune. Following are a couple of ways to check its placement:

1. **Measurement**. The 12th fret should be exactly halfway between the nut and the bridge. Carefully measure the distance from the nut to the 12th fret (measure to the fret wire itself), and then measure the distance from the 12th fret to the bridge. The two distances should be equal. If you need to move the bridge, hold the banjo in your lap and grip the bridge between the thumb and index fingers of both hands. Then, gently slide the bridge toward or away from the neck until the measurement from the 12th fret to the bridge is the same as from the 12th fret to the nut. This method will get you very close, but for more accuracy, it's best to set the bridge using harmonics.

Measuring the bridge placement.

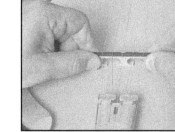
Moving the bridge.

2. **Harmonics**. *Harmonics* are pure, clear tones produced by picking the string while gently touching it at a specific division of the string length, usually the 12th fret. With harmonics, you don't fret the string in the traditional way. Rather, you barely touch the string just over the fret wire, pick the string, and then immediately let go after picking. You should hear a bell-like chime, which is a harmonic. Once you're able to play the harmonic, compare the note that you hear with the fretted note at the same fret. If the fretted note is sharp (slightly higher than the harmonic), then you'll need to move the bridge back toward the tailpiece. If the fretted note is flat (lower than the harmonic), then you'll need to move the bridge forward (toward the neck). You probably won't have to move it very far. Move the bridge in the manner described above.

Finger touching the string at the 12th fret to produce a harmonic.

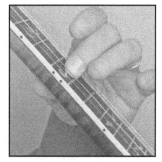
Finger depressing the string at the 12th fret to test the tuning and bridge placement.

The bridge usually only moves if it's been bumped or deliberately moved, but it's a good idea to check the intonation as described above if the tuning on the banjo has changed significantly (often a sign that it's been bumped).

ADJUSTING THE ACTION

On a string instrument, the *action* refers to the playability of the instrument related to the height of the strings off of the fretboard. A *lower action* (strings closer to the fretboard) makes the instrument easier to play, but if it's too low, the strings can vibrate against the frets and cause a buzz. There are two adjustments that can easily be made on your banjo to lower or raise the action. If you are unsure about trying this yourself, or aren't that comfortable with the idea, take it to a repair shop. If you want to check it out yourself, there are specific things to look for.

Check the neck *relief,* or curvature. Contrary to what you may have heard, the neck should not be perfectly straight. You can check this by holding the 3rd string down at the 1st fret (or place a capo at the 1st fret), and then holding the same string down at the highest fret (probably the 22nd). Now look at the string from the side and see if there is any space between the top of the 10th fret and the string. If the string is touching the fret, your neck is too straight or possibly bowed backward. There should be a gap of about 1/64" (between 0.010" and 0.015"), or just a little less space than the thickness of your 4th string. If the gap is bigger than that, your neck is bowed forward.

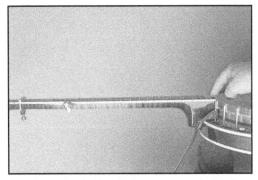

Test the neck relief by placing a capo at the 1st fret and fretting at the highest fret.

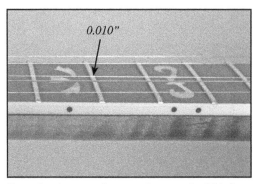

Example of proper clearance between the 10th fret and the string.

Neck relief can be adjusted with the *truss rod,* which is an adjustable metal rod inside the banjo neck that is usually accessible through a small cover held in place by two screws on the front of the headstock, as shown below. Under this cover is a small cavity with a truss-rod nut that should be adjustable with a nut driver or an allen wrench.

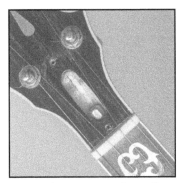

Truss rod cover removed revealing truss rod nut.

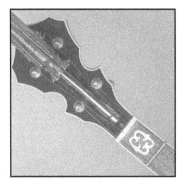

Nut driver adjusting truss rod.

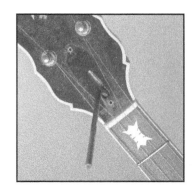

Allen wrench adjusting truss rod.

If your banjo neck is too straight, loosen the truss rod by turning the nut counterclockwise. If the neck is too bowed, tighten the nut by turning it clockwise. The truss rod is meant to make minor adjustments only. If your neck needs to be adjusted by more than 1/4", take it to a qualified repair shop.

Now that you've checked that your bridge is in the correct place and that the truss rod is properly adjusted, measure the height of the strings above the highest fret (22nd) to find out the distance between the bottom of the string and the top of the fret wire.

Measuring string height at the 22nd fret.

If the distance is 1/8" or less, your action is very low. Low action will make it very easy to play, but may cause the strings to buzz against the fretboard. If your strings are higher than 1/4" off of the 22nd fret, you have high action. If you play very loud, striking the strings hard, high action will help keep the strings from buzzing, but it could also be a bit difficult to play. The ideal range is between 1/8" and 1/4". You will most likely not need to make an adjustment if your action is around there. You can adjust your action with the *coordinator rods*, which are located inside the rim of your banjo. (They also serve the purpose of holding the neck onto the pot of the banjo.) There are three common types of coordinator-rod systems.*

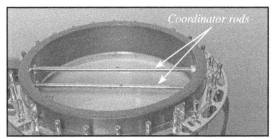

Banjo with two coordinator rods.

Coordinator rod and lag-bolt nut.

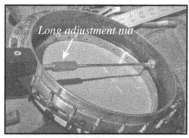

Aluminum rim banjo with single rod and long adjustment nut.

BANJOS WITH ONE OR TWO COORDINATOR RODS

Most professional-grade banjos (and banjos designed like them) have two coordinator rods that serve to hold the neck in place and adjust the action. One rod is closest to the head, while the other is closest to the back of the banjo. The single-rod system looks the same except the rod closest to the head is replaced by a single nut that holds the neck bolt in place.

The procedure for adjusting the action is the same for both of these systems. First, check to see if the rods are tight and that none of the nuts are loose. The rod closest to the back of the banjo will have a nut on either side of the rim as shown in the photo.

To lower the action: Loosen the nut on the inside of the banjo rim and slowly tighten the nut on the outside. Check the action again after about a half turn, and see if any more tightening is needed. If so, turn it about another half turn and check again. If you have turned the nut more than a whole turn and no change in the action has occurred, take the banjo to a repair shop to make sure there is not other damage. If the action is set where you want it, tighten the inside nut, double-check the nut on the front rod (make sure it isn't loose), and you should be ready to go.

To raise the action: Loosen the nut on the outside of the banjo rim and tighten the nut on the inside. As in the instructions above, check after every half turn of the nut. Once the desired change is made, tighten the outside nut, double-check the nut on the front rod, put your banjo back together, and start picking!

* Some banjos (especially home-made ones) may have a different system than the ones shown. If you encounter this, seek out the builder, owner's manual, or a repair shop for assistance.

ALUMINUM RIM, SINGLE-ROD "LONG NUT" ADJUSTMENT

It is very common for beginning instruments to have just one coordinator rod that attaches to the single bolt coming down from the neck. A long nut, as shown in the photo on page 87, attaches the coordinator rod to the neck bolt. This is perhaps the easiest of all to adjust. Tightening the rod (turning it clockwise) lowers the action; loosening it (counterclockwise) raises the action. You'll also notice the banjo's tuning will change drastically with this adjustment. This is normal. Make sure the bolt holding the neck to the pot is secure, and adjust until the strings are at the proper height.

TIGHTENING THE HEAD

The head on your banjo can also be adjusted to change the sound. If the head is loose, the banjo can sound dull or "tubby." Tightening the head can make it sound brighter and sharper. This adjustment is not difficult but over-tightening the head can cause it to break, so use caution. To tighten the head, remove the resonator and find a wrench or nut driver that fits the nuts on the bottom of the hooks that hold the head in place. First, check to see if any of the nuts are loose. If so, tighten them just enough to keep them in place and then, starting with the nut next to the neck, give each one about a quarter turn. When you've gone all the way around, give the banjo a listen. If you like it, keep it there. If you think you'd like it a little brighter, try another quarter turn. Keep looking at the tension hoop (see below) to make sure that you've tightened the head evenly all the way around.

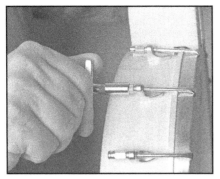

Tightening the banjo head.

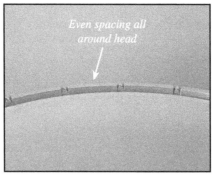

Even spacing between the rim and hoop, all the way around the head.

CHANGING THE HEAD

If you ever need to change your banjo head, the process is close to the steps above. You'll need to loosen all of the hooks and nuts, remove the old head, and then replace it with a new one. Banjo heads can be made of different materials and come in different styles, but most modern banjo heads are made out of plastic (mylar) and don't wear out very easily. Unless you're really curious about something different, the old adage holds true: "If it ain't broke, don't fix it."

LESSON 3: CHANGING STRINGS

Of all the maintenance items you'll need to do on your banjo, changing the strings is probably the most important and frequent one. Knowing how to change the strings properly will help you stay in tune and keep your banjo sounding its best.

Why change strings? In order to play in tune, a string must vibrate evenly along its entire length. Banjo strings are made of steel and though they are fairly corrosion-resistant, they do get rusty, dirty, and even slightly bent and deformed by the wear on the fret wires. Once this happens, the strings will no longer vibrate evenly, making them harder to stay in tune. How often you'll need to change is dependent on a few factors, including how many hours you play each day, how sweaty your hands are, how hard you pick, and even the kind of strings you use. For most of us who play every day, changing strings once a month—or maybe every two months—is a good idea. Waiting till six months is pushing it, and a year is too long. Some professionals change strings as often as every week (and sometimes more!).

Change your strings one at a time. If you remove all the strings, the bridge will come off, the tailpiece will come loose, and you'll be completely out of tune. By changing one at a time, you can use the other strings as a guide and tune the new string to them as well.

Let's start with the 1st string. Look at how the other strings are attached at the tailpiece, and you'll see how to attach the new one. Banjo strings usually have loop ends. Slip the loop end of the string over the hook or pin, and make sure the new string is following the same path as the other strings.

Tailpiece with strings attached.

Turn the 1st-string tuner so that the hole in the post runs parallel to the fretboard. Keep holding the string so that it does not come loose from the tailpiece, and thread the string through the hole in the tuner post. Leave enough slack so that the string will go around the post two or three times, and leave enough space between the string and the fretboard to get your hand between them as shown in the picture at the right.

Take the end of the string and loop it around the tuner post, under the slack end of the string as shown in the photo. For the 1st and 2nd strings, loop the string counterclockwise. For the 3rd, 4th, and 5th strings, loop clockwise.

Bend the loose end around the slack end of the string, so that it will wrap over itself once the tuner starts winding, then start turning the tuner to wrap the string around the post. The tuner post should wind clockwise for the 1st and 2nd strings, and counterclockwise for the 3rd, 4th, and 5th strings.

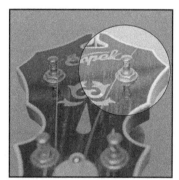

String going through tuner post, leaving slack.

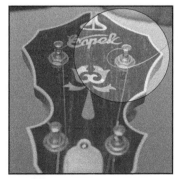

String looped around the tuner post and bent upward.

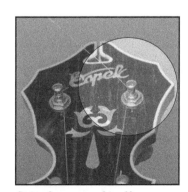

String bent around itself.

String being wound around the tuning post.

STRING GAUGE

The *gauge* of the string refers to the diameter or thickness of the wire. The numbers are usually given in thousandths of an inch. For example, a 10-gauge string is .010". The higher-pitched strings on your banjo are thinner, while the lower-pitched strings are heavier. On most banjos, the 4th string is *wound*—the string is made up of two very thin strings, a thin core wire and a thinner wire wrapped around it to make the string thicker without an increase in tension.

As a general rule, the heavier the gauge, the more difficult it is to hold down the strings. A heavier wire, when tuned to the same pitch, is under greater tension. Most banjo strings are sold as either medium or light gauge. Unless you play very hard, light gauge is probably fine (many professionals use light-gauge strings). You may also notice there isn't truly a standard when it comes to labeling them as light or medium. One brand may sell a light set that uses the same gauges as another brand's medium. Try a few brands until you find one you like.

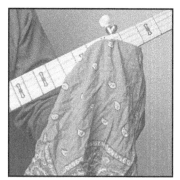

Wiping the strings clean with a bandana.

One way to keep your strings fresh is to keep them clean. Keep a rag, bandana, or soft cloth in your case, and wipe the strings off every time you are done playing. A cotton handkerchief or bandana works well; terrycloth towels or soft flannel can leave lint and threads behind. There are products available that claim to clean and lubricate your strings, but simply wiping the strings clean works pretty well and doesn't leave a greasy residue.

LESSON 4: KEEPING YOUR BANJO CLEAN

Along with keeping the strings clean, it's good practice to wipe the entire banjo neck clean after playing. Keeping your banjo clean and wiped-off between playing sessions is a good way to keep it looking good. Remember, a protective finish, such as lacquer, varnish, or polyurethane, covers most of the wooden parts of your banjo, so if there is something sticky on the finish or a bad smudge, a slightly damp cloth and a little elbow grease will usually do the trick. Before using any instrument or furniture polish, make sure you read the label and know what sort of finish is on your instrument. Some types of furniture wax can have an adverse reaction to the lacquer or varnish. Also, keep your banjo in its case when you are not playing to help keep it free from dust.

Your banjo head is most likely made out of plastic or mylar. Most white banjo heads are sprayed with a lightly textured coating to keep it from being too smooth (although some are smooth and even clear). To keep a conventional, frosted banjo head clean, you can use an over-the-counter spray cleaner (like window cleaner). Since the head is plastic, you're not going to hurt it, but try not to over spray and get the cleaning solution on any of the wooden parts. For scuffs marks, a pencil eraser will do a pretty good job.

LESSON 5: BANJO STRAPS

TYPES OF STRAPS

Banjo straps come in a few different varieties. The least expensive straps are usually cloth with a plastic or vinyl backing. Some of these straps have a metal hook for attaching to the banjo. Be careful with these straps, as the metal hook can scratch the banjo finish. If you can't find an actual banjo strap, a little creativity with a guitar strap can do the trick.

Leather banjo strap.

Cloth banjo strap.

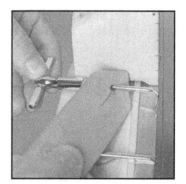

Guitar strap attached as banjo strap.

ATTACHING A BANJO STRAP

Most often, the banjo strap is attached to the bracket hooks that hold the banjo head in place. The strap may be attached either above or below the neck (as shown) with the other end attached to a bracket hook near the tailpiece.

Banjo strap attached above the neck.

Banjo strap attached below the neck.

Banjo strap attached near the tailpiece.

To install the strap, remove the resonator, then remove the nut that holds the bracket hook in place. Slide the hook through the hole in the strap and put the nut back on. Get the nut finger-tight, and then add an eighth to a quarter turn more to ensure that it stays in place. Adjust the height to a comfortable position. If the strap is too long, the banjo will be too low and you'll have to extend your hands to reach the neck.

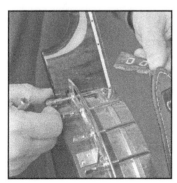

Removing bracket hook.

Threading bracket hook through the strap.

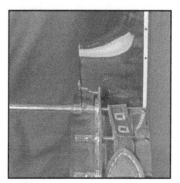

Tightening the bracket hook.

APPENDIX

Practice every day! Any music teacher or musician will confirm that practicing every day is the best way to progress on an instrument. Even 10 to 15 minutes every day is better than a whole hour every three or four days. This is because you are not only learning new information, but you're acquiring new physical skills. It will be easier to develop the muscle memory in your hands and fingers (not to mention building calluses on your fretting hand) if you practice every day. Aim for at least 30 minutes a day.

WHAT TO PRACTICE

When you're first getting started, your practice will be limited to carefully repeating whatever you've learned so far, but once you've learned a few tunes and techniques, here's how you can structure a 30–40 minute practice session:

1. **10 minutes: Warm up**. Play a few easy things, like rolls (possibly while changing chords), and maybe an easy tune or two, just to get your fingers warmed up.

2. **15–20 minutes: Current project**. Use this time to focus on the current section of the book you are working on, or current tune or song that you are learning. If you go over the allotted time for this—even better!

3. **5–10 minutes: Review**. Use this time to go back and play through the last couple of tunes or techniques you've learned. Use this time to refine your technique and sound.

WHERE AND WHEN TO PRACTICE

The answer to when and where you practice will depend on your schedule and lifestyle, but as a general rule, if you can find a specific time every day to devote to practice, it will help make the banjo a part of your daily routine. If you're an early bird, maybe get your half hour in before breakfast. If you're more of a night owl, try doing it just before bed (just make sure no one is trying to sleep nearby!).

The best place to practice is somewhere free from distractions. Turn off your phone and TV! In fact, if you're looking for time to devote to the banjo, just try giving up 30 minutes of TV watching per day. You may be surprised how little you miss it! If your mind is racing with other thoughts, or other problems, it can be difficult to get started. So try to be relaxed before you begin. If you can't, then take care of the other problems and try to come back to the banjo when your head is clear. Distracted practice isn't much better than no practice at all (but it is still better).

RECORD YOURSELF

When you are focused on playing a certain lick or a new tune, it's easy to become too involved in the details of what you are doing and lose sight of the overall sound. Recording yourself and then listening back will allow you to hear what you've played the way another person hears it. Doing this will help you to listen more objectively while you're playing. It's also a good way to track your progress. Nowadays, you can record yourself easily with your computer or smart phone. There are also many inexpensive digital recorders on the market. If you have an old tape recorder lying around, you can dust it off and use that.

METRONOME

A metronome is an adjustable mechanical or electrical device that produces a sound at a steady, selectable tempo for keeping a steady beat. A metronome will produce a click or other sound at regular intervals usually measured in beats per minute (*BPM*). A metronome setting of 60 BPM would be one beat every second. The classic mechanical metronome that many are familiar with is the pyramid shaped, pendulum-style device that is often seen on top of a piano. The weight on the pendulum is moved up and down to adjust the tempo. Mechanical metronomes often require winding like an old-fashioned clock and, in fact, many were made by clock manufacturers. Electronic metronomes either plug in or run on batteries and have either a dial or digital display for choosing the tempo. There are even metronome apps for smartphones.

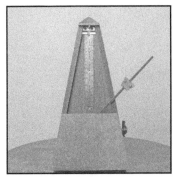

Pendulum metronome.

Electronic metronome.

Practicing with a metronome will help you develop a good sense of time and a steady rhythm when you play. Many musicians have a love/hate relationship with the metronome. When you first start to play with one, it's not unusual to think that the metronome is speeding up or slowing down. It takes some practice, but here are a few tips for starting with the metronome:

- Start by playing something simple, like basic rolls. Trying to play a whole song with the metronome can be frustrating, so start by playing a roll or a very simple tune. Try to tap your foot and feel the tempo that is comfortable for you, then set the metronome to that tempo and play along with it. Some metronomes have a tap-tempo feature that allows you to establish the tempo by tapping on it. Once you've gotten comfortable with playing a roll, move on to a simple song or passage and work up from there.
- At very slow tempos, set the metronome at double speed. To play the alternating roll below (Ex. 106) at a tempo of 60 BPM, the metronome should only click when the 3rd and 4th strings are played. By setting the metronome twice as fast to 120 BPM (Ex. 107), the click will be heard every time the 3rd, 4th, and 5th strings are played, giving you twice as many beats to keep in time with.

106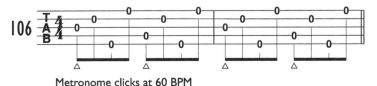

Metronome clicks at 60 BPM

107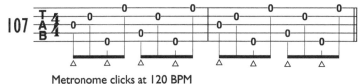

Metronome clicks at 120 BPM

LISTEN, LISTEN, LISTEN!

This may seem obvious, but to be a good banjo player, you'll need to know what banjo music is supposed to sound like, and the only way to do that is to listen! Listening will not only teach you what the music is supposed to sound like, but will also help inspire you to play more. The 5-string banjo is finding its way into all kinds of music today, from traditional mountain folk music, to classical, jazz, country, bluegrass, and even rock. Below is a list of a few notable banjo greats in a few different categories. Seek out their recordings and listen. Keep an open mind and remember that many of the most progressive and innovative players of today spent a lot of time listening to the original pioneers. Also, remember that the original pioneers, who we may think of as traditional now, were probably pretty progressive and innovative in their day. Bear in mind that many of these players could easily be placed in more than one category.

BLUEGRASS

Tom Adams
Eddie Adcock
Kristin Scott Benson
J. D. Crowe
Bill Keith
Jim Mills
Alan Munde
Sonny Osborne
Don Reno
Earl Scruggs
Sammy Shelor
Ralph Stanley

PROGRESSIVE BLUEGRASS: NEWGRASS

Danny Barnes
Alison Brown
Bill Evans
Béla Fleck
Courtney Johnson
Mike Munford
Chris Pandolfi
Noam Pikelny
Tony Trischka
Scott Vestal

OLD-TIME: CLAWHAMMER

Cathy Fink
Tommy Jarrell
Grandpa Jones
Mark Johnson
Dan Levenson
Reed Martin
Michael J. Miles
Joe Newberry
Ken Perlman

JAZZ

Alison Brown
Ryan Cavanaugh
Pat Cloud
Béla Fleck

FOLK

Dave Guard (Kingston Trio)
John Hartford
Mike Seeger
Pete Seeger

CLASSICAL

John Bullard
Béla Fleck
Michael J. Miles
Jake Schepps

RAGTIME

Clarke Buehling
Bill Knopf

OTHER LISTENING RESOURCES

Internet and satellite radio both offer channels that program bluegrass, folk, and other acoustic music choices. Listen, take notes of the bands and players that you like, and then spend some time seeking out their music. You may find audio and even video of your favorite players online but for the real, in-depth experience, get the complete albums. You may find deeper catalog stuff that you'll like even better.

GO SEE LIVE MUSIC!

There's nothing quite like the excitement of a live music experience. If one of your favorite players is coming to town or appearing at a music festival, make plans to go see them. Not only is it inspirational, you'll get a good look at their hands and maybe get some insight on how they do it. And go see some local banjo players, too. There's probably a pretty good one not far from you. Maybe they'll even give you some pointers!

CONCLUSION

Congratulations on completing *Beginning Banjo*! We've covered a lot in this volume, and you are now on your way to becoming a well-rounded banjo player. With the skills you've learned so far, you might be asking yourself what's next? The next step is to learn how to improvise and create your own solos to songs, and that's the focus of the next book in this series, *Intermediate Banjo*. There, we'll learn how to make up solos for chord progressions using standard bluegrass licks. We'll learn how to use moveable chord shapes and double-stop positions to improvise "on the fly," and we'll work on up-the-neck playing (playing solos to songs in a higher register up the neck). *Intermediate Banjo* also includes lessons on advanced melodic-style playing (including playing melodic style in different keys), more backup playing, single-string style, and lots more.

Keep practicing what you've learned here, and we'll see you soon in *Intermediate Banjo*!